ACTIVE START
FOR
HEALTHY KIDS

· · · · · · · · ·

Activities, Exercises, and Nutritional Tips

Stephen J. Virgilio, PhD

Human Kinetics

Library of Congress Cataloging-in-Publication Data

Virgilio, Stephen J.
  Active start for healthy kids : activities, exercises, and nutritional tips / Stephen J. Virgilio.
    p. cm.
  Includes bibliographical references.
  ISBN 0-7360-5281-X (soft cover : alk. paper)
  1. Exercise for children. 2. Physical fitness for children. 3. Sports for children. 4. Children--Nutrition. 5. Children--Health and hygiene. 6. Family recreation. 7. Games. I. Title.
  RJ133.V54 2005
  613.7'042--dc22

                                                                                        2005012484

ISBN-10: 0-7360-5281-X
ISBN-13: 978-0-7360-5281-8

Acquisitions Editor: Scott Wikgren; **Developmental Editor:** Ray Vallese; **Assistant Editor:** Derek Campbell; **Copyeditor:** Barb Field; **Proofreader:** Julie Marx Goodreau; **Permission Manager:** Dalene Reeder; **Graphic Designer:** Fred Starbird; **Graphic Artist:** Angela K. Snyder; **Photo Managers:** Dan Wendt and Sarah Ritz; **Cover Designer:** Keith Blomberg; **Photographer (front and back covers):** Kelly J. Huff; **Photographer (interior):** Kelly J. Huff, unless otherwise noted; **Art Manager:** Kelly Hendren; **Illustrator:** Al Wilborn; **Printer:** Versa Press

Printed in the United States of America

10 9 8 7 6 5 4 3 2

Human Kinetics
Web site: www.HumanKinetics.com
United States: Human Kinetics
P.O. Box 5076
Champaign, IL 61825-5076
800-747-4457
e-mail: humank@hkusa.com

Canada: Human Kinetics
475 Devonshire Road Unit 100
Windsor, ON N8Y 2L5
800-465-7301 (in Canada only)
e-mail: orders@hkcanada.com

Europe: Human Kinetics
107 Bradford Road
Stanningley
Leeds LS28 6AT, United Kingdom
+44 (0) 113 255 5665
e-mail: hk@hkeurope.com

Australia: Human Kinetics
57A Price Avenue
Lower Mitcham, South Australia 5062
08 8277 1555
e-mail: liaw@hkaustralia.com

New Zealand: Human Kinetics
Division of Sports Distributors NZ Ltd.
P.O. Box 300 226 Albany
North Shore City
Auckland
0064 9 448 1207
e-mail: info@humankinetics.co.nz

To my wife, Irene

Contents

Activity Finder

Preface

"If a child is to keep alive his inborn sense of wonder, he needs the companionship of at least one adult who can share it, rediscovering with him the joy, excitement, and mystery of the world we live in." —Rachel Carson

Young children love to move. They are born with an instinct for physical activity—running, playing, jumping, dancing, and so on. So why then are childhood obesity levels at epidemic proportions in this country?

According to the Centers for Disease Control and Prevention (2002), the number of overweight and obese children in the United States has more than doubled over the last 20 years. Studies also show that children become less active as they move from elementary school into junior high school. What has happened to the youth of our nation over the past two decades?

As a society, we "dropped the ball." Preoccupied with our fast-paced, hectic lifestyles and immersed in a pop culture of fast-food chains and sedentary recreational pursuits, we paid little attention to the long-term importance of physical activity and healthy eating habits to the mental, social, emotional, and physical well-being of our children. The result is a generation of young people obsessed with eating and glued to their TV and computer screens. Children today spend about eight hours per day sitting, at least four hours of that time watching TV and playing video games. Unfortunately, the evidence also suggests that children who are overweight and sedentary have a 70% chance of continuing this pattern well into adulthood (Ogden et al. 2002). What must be done to reverse this pattern?

I have been researching and teaching about issues surrounding children's health for more than 25 years. In the late 1980s, I codeveloped and coauthored the nationally known Heart Smart Program (Berenson et al. 1998d), a comprehensive health intervention project aimed at changing the eating and physical activity behaviors of children in grades K-6. The Heart Smart approach was designed around an all-inclusive home, school, and community model. The intent was to effect changes in a child's total learning environment that would set the conditions for positive long-term healthy lifestyle behaviors.

The results of this study and the experience I gained from working with teachers, physicians, politicians, parents, and community leaders have given me cause for hope. I truly believe that the obesity epidemic is reversible in our lifetime, but it's going to take a team effort. When the Heart Smart Program model approach is fully adopted on a national scale, we will see remarkable results.

A significant finding of my work was the impact of early intervention on children's health behaviors. The Heart Smart model was designed to reach elementary schoolchildren before they develop health-compromising behaviors later in life. Therefore, what might be the impact on long-term health habits if we could reach the preschool population? That would be true prevention.

My work continued into the 1990s with a renewed interest in and passion for toddlers and preschoolers, but took a different path. Rather than focusing on play, expressive movement, and social interaction as the benefits of physical activity, I taught and wrote about how these positive characteristics help shape a child's body image, enhance self-concept, nurture an appreciation for physical activity, and establish proper eating habits for weight control that will last a lifetime.

Based on my work in the Heart Smart Program, I realized that lifestyle behaviors should be developed early in life and that it would take a team effort to obtain the maximum results. Thus, the premise of this book is based on two important benchmarks:

- An early start: Children experiencing and learning the benefits of physical activity and healthful living at ages two through six will develop positive behaviors that may last well into adulthood.

- Team effort: No one parent, grandparent, teacher, caregiver, or physician can do it alone. To have a lasting effect on our children's health, we need the help of the people children value most in their lives.

This book is intended to be a resource for all who interact with children ages two through six. Chapter 1 offers suggestions for heightening awareness about the problem of childhood obesity and the importance of children being physically active, and chapter 2 presents a new physical activity pyramid as well as physical activity guidelines for young children. Chapter 3 provides nutrition guidelines based on the U.S. Department of Agriculture (USDA) Food Guide Pyramid for Young Children ages two through six and discusses the possibilities for striking a balance between physical activity choices and eating habits. It also includes guidelines for changing the eating behaviors of children, as well as healthy recipes that children enjoy.

Chapter 4 offers suggestions for fun family activities, and chapters 5 though 9 present numerous developmentally appropriate exercises, games, dance and rhythm activities, movement skills, and yoga poses for young children. Each activity description includes the intended age level, designated according to the developmental stages (ages two to three and ages four to six), and the objectives, equipment and materials needed, and modifications.

Incorporate these fun and exciting activities into a child's day—every day. However, take note of the developmental concerns and guidelines that are included in the introduction to each chapter. Simply stated, *how* you teach children a physical activity is as important as the activity itself.

Remember, your enthusiasm for, support for, and understanding of the importance of physical activity and sound eating habits will help guide the next generation of youngsters toward a lifetime of good health.

Now let's all take action—together!

Acknowledgments

First and foremost, I would like to thank my wife Irene for her love and unwavering support throughout this project. Also, deep gratitude goes to my two sons Stephen and Joseph for the love and inspiration you give me each day. As young men, you have already far exceeded my wildest dreams and expectations. To my parents Joseph and Marianne, thank you for showing me the most precious responsibility in life—parenting.

To my students at Adelphi University, thank you very much for your help in experimenting and researching the many activities found in this book. I would also like to acknowledge my devoted graduate assistants, Andrea Smith and Barbara Olsen—you were a big help. Special thanks to Nicole Bove, my research assistant, for her feedback, creativity, and encouragement during the developmental stages of this book.

I would also like to acknowledge the many fine professionals that participated in my workshops and seminars over the last three years and encouraged me to write this book. Appreciation goes to the teachers from The Illinois Resource Center for Early Childhood; The Women, Infants, and Children (WIC) Association of NY State; and the NY State Department of Health, Eat Well—Play Hard program. You showed me the way—thank you.

Many thanks to the models who posed for the photographs in this book: Allec Bryan, Aidan Erb-Wilson, Emily Graves, Jake Gulick, Lauren Henderson, Dana Herman, Cade Hettmansberger, Cole Hettmansberger, Kelly Maloney, Alexander Muzinic, Connor Muzinic, Makayla Muzinic, Madelyn Ronk, Jessica Rose, Gloria Sunderland, Lisa Swanson, Olivia Swanson, Jordyn Tietz, and Brantley Virgilio.

Finally, I would like to extend my gratitude to all the professionals at Human Kinetics who worked so diligently on this book. Special thanks to Scott Wikgren, division director, who shared my concern about the serious issues surrounding childhood obesity and had the courage to support a publication concerning the need for early intervention in young children before the age of six. Big thanks to Ray Vallese, my editor. I am grateful for your attention to detail, as well as your insights, contributions, and questions. Working closely with such quality individuals as Scott Wikgren and Ray Vallese made this project a truly rewarding experience.

Chapter 1

© Human Kinetics

LET'S GET STARTED TOGETHER

The current generation of children throughout the world is at risk for a problem far more serious than youth violence, drug abuse, environmental hazards, terrorism, or HIV infection. The major problem facing children today is obesity. The obesity issue is so serious that unless trends are reversed over the next several years, experts predict that the current generation of American children will be the first to live shorter lives than their parents (U.S. Department of Health and Human Services 2000).

Physical inactivity and poor eating habits have contributed to the nation's epidemic of childhood obesity. The current statistics are staggering and have raised serious concerns for the future of this country. According to studies conducted by the Centers for Disease Control and Prevention (CDC) (2002), the percentage of children ages 6 through 19 who are overweight has doubled since 1980. Over 15% of the children in this age category are overweight or obese. Among this population, 61% have one or more cardiovascular disease risk factors and 27% have two or more. The long-term effects of obesity translate into significant risk of heart disease; colon, stomach, and breast cancer; hypertension; type 2 diabetes; and osteoarthritis. The outlook is dim, but regular **physical activity** may alleviate the risk of these illnesses.

Benefits of Regular Physical Activity

- Reduces the risk of dying prematurely
- Reduces the risk of heart disease
- Reduces the risk of developing diabetes
- Reduces the risk of developing high blood pressure
- Reduces blood pressure in people who already have elevated readings
- Reduces the risk of colon cancer
- Helps control weight
- Helps build and maintain healthy bones, muscles, and joints
- Promotes psychological well-being

— CDC 1996

Childhood obesity has become everyone's problem. The downward cycle will only get worse unless all involved accept responsibility, take action, and begin to reverse these trends. The government needs to establish better policies to support child health. Preschool and kindergarten programs need to include physical education curriculum content and provide opportunities for physical activity every day. Parents must assume responsibility for the health and well-being of their children by planning healthy meals and supporting physical activity as a positive way to stay healthy and have fun. Finally, communities throughout the nation should understand the importance of establishing active environments for children. For instance, according to a 2003 Gallup survey, less than half of American children have a playground within walking distance of their homes.

The well-being of children from infancy through teenage years has been improved in other areas, however. Infant and childhood death rates continue to drop. Fewer adolescents are smoking, and fewer are exposed to secondhand smoke. Thanks to the widespread use of vaccines, mumps, measles, and rubella are rare. Seat belts and infant car seats, as well as safer car designs, have significantly reduced the number of fatalities and injuries on the road. Unfortunately, far less attention has been directed at children's physical activity levels and eating behaviors. The obesity epidemic has become so serious it threatens to significantly reduce other improvements in children's health and safety during the last three decades (National Center for Health Statistics 2004). This book will focus on two of the most important concerns surrounding childhood obesity:

- Establishing patterns of daily physical activity. One goal of this book is to provide you with a valuable resource for incorporating safe, fun, and developmentally appropriate physical activity into a child's day for ages two through six.
- Healthy eating habits. Another goal is to suggest healthy recipes, snacking ideas, and fun activities that integrate nutrition concepts, as well as guidelines to help control weight.

Both go hand in hand and are essential to establishing a positive healthy lifestyle in young children. Positive trends are starting to develop. School-based programs and new community initiatives are surfacing throughout the nation. Parents are becoming better informed about how to read nutrition labels, and big business is finally getting the message—fast-food chains are now offering healthy food choices along with the traditional burgers and fries.

Many of the new approaches, however, fail to focus on the young child, ages two through six. What about eating habits? Is anyone monitoring a child's activity levels? Where are the intervention programs in pre-schools? Is big business paying any attention to the three-year-old? The eating habits and activity levels of children ages two through six have been overlooked for many years. The general mind-set was "Children are healthy—they don't get heart disease or cancer." Or "They seem active. Why worry about the amount or type of physical activity they are get-ting?" Or "They are only kids. Let them have candy and cake. It makes them happy." Sound familiar? What about a trip to the grandparents for a visit? "The children look so thin, so unhealthy—they need a few more pounds. Leave them with me for a week!"

Many other obstacles exist. Our fast-paced lifestyle has created eating habits that are dangerous to the health of young children. Processed, prepackaged food, microwave meals, stops at the local fast-food restau-rant, high-fat sugary snacks, and consumption of too many calories have contributed to the current health issues of children. TV, video games, DVD players, and computers have all led to a generation of desk jockeys at preschools during the day and couch potatoes at home in the evening.

According to the *Healthy People 2010* report (U.S. Department of Health and Human Services 2000), the future health problems facing young children are substantial and call for immediate action. This book offers solutions, strategies for change, and practical ideas for getting children moving and eating well.

PHYSICAL ACTIVITY FOR YOUNG CHILDREN: A PHILOSOPHY

My philosophy focuses on creating positive health habits in young children for long-term benefits and is based on five principles.

1. Children should be taught the health benefits of physical activity and proper eating habits. Chapter 2, as well as the numerous activities in the book, will further illustrate this principle.

2. Physical activity is for everyone. All children are entitled to the healthful benefits of physical activity, **play**, games, dance, and sport. Children with disabilities, including obese children, are often ignored and are not provided the same opportunities to move as other children. Pay close attention to the "Modifications" section of the activity descriptions for ways to include these children in activities.

3. Physical activity should be reinforced through a child's innate desire to move. All children begin life with an innate need and desire to play and move. Teachers, caregivers, and parents should continue to promote this need in a positive, noncompetitive environment on a daily basis.

4. Good health habits should be fun. Physical activity and eating with friends, classmates, and family should take place in a relaxed, safe, supportive environment. Children should have fun when they are physically active—laughing, singing, moving, and exploring. Positive experiences will reinforce the continued desire to move. Children should also have fun when they are eating. Make meals colorful, create food designs, and make eating a family affair.

5. Children should be taught in a manner that is appropriate for children. They are not miniature adults. Many of the approaches and techniques adults identify with are inappropriate for young children, such as maintaining a workout schedule or routine and measuring weekly gains. For many years, we taught children based on the premise that their motivations to move were similar to those of adults. Children are physically active because they enjoy play, need to interact with their peers, want to develop new motor skills, and need to express themselves through physical activity. Furthermore, their eating habits are quite different. For example, children normally eat about every 2 1/2 hours throughout the day, or five or six smaller meals per day (Insel et al. 2003).

This philosophy is put into practice using the two major approaches mentioned in the preface: giving kids an early start and using a team approach to accomplish your goals.

Early Start

By giving children an early start, I do not mean preparing children to become elite athletes. The early start should begin with a strong infusion of the philosophical principles discussed earlier. An early start is intended to help youngsters develop certain attitudes, beliefs, and behaviors that will help establish a set of core values about a healthy lifestyle. According to the National Association for Sport and Physical Education (NASPE) (2002), the preschool level is ideal for establishing healthful behavior—the earlier, the better. Changing children's attitudes about physical activity and eating patterns gets more difficult once they have reached their teens.

Many parents, however, view their child's physical activity time as preparation for athletics. This mind-set has caused serious problems. Children are not miniature Yankees or Giants or Lakers—they are children. Children ages two through six are not developmentally ready for team sports and competition. Here's why.

- Mentally, they are ill-equipped to process the complexities of a sport competition.
- According to developmental psychology, children ages two through six are unable to discriminate between a losing game and their own self-worth.
- Parents and coaches emphasize winning as the main goal—adding unnecessary stress to an activity.
- Children do not have the necessary motor skills to participate successfully in a competitive sport. Although age two through age six is an excellent time to develop motor skills, parents and coaches spend too much time on game skills rather than on individual motor skills.
- Children are more susceptible to overuse injuries due to a lack of muscular strength to support major joints. They are also prone to injuries due to a lack of coordination and depth perception.

Giving kids an early start in developmentally appropriate physical activity, however, will provide them with a foundation for a healthy lifestyle and with the necessary motor skills to serve as building blocks for more advanced motor skills, games, and sport activity later in life.

Teaching children to be competent movers will open many doors of opportunity throughout their lives. Most important, children will appreciate the joy of movement and what it can accomplish in their mental, physical, or social development.

A Team Approach: Together Everyone Achieves More

The second consideration is the team approach. Many experts agree that significant changes in a child's eating and physical activity habits are unlikely unless a strong relationship exists among the home, school, and community (Virgilio 1997). A cardiovascular health intervention model called the Heart Smart Program (Berenson et al. 1998d) produced positive results in the eating and physical activity behaviors of children at the elementary school level by developing a comprehensive approach. The model included intervention strategies for the home, school, and community. A similar model is needed at the preschool level to ensure long-term behavior changes (see figure 1.1).

Home

The family unit is the most powerful influence on a child's health and physical activity patterns. If children are to develop positive long-term behaviors, parents must serve as key members of the team. Parental involvement can be encouraged through three basic strategies: parent education, parent participation, and home-based activities.

Parent Education

Prekindergarten (Pre-K) centers and elementary schools should help provide parents with up-to-date health and physical activity information. Parents must know the "hows" and "whys" before they will begin to help promote their child's health.

Here are several ideas:

- Newsletters: Develop an eye-catching format with graphics. Each newsletter should have a theme such as "Yoga: Make it a Family Affair." The newsletter may also be used for announcements, updates, safety hints, and fun family activities.
- Parent seminars: The Pre-K center or elementary school could schedule monthly health seminars through Parent-Teacher Association (PTA) meetings, early-bird sessions, or during lunchtime.

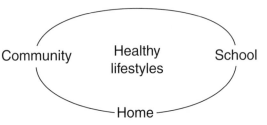

Figure 1.1—Diagram of the team approach—home, school, community.

- Progress report: Keep parents up to date with height and weight data and what specific physical activities children are engaged in throughout the school year.
- PTA demo: Arrange to have children perform exercise routines, including dance and singing activities. Invite a health professional to speak and include a few handouts or brochures from national associations such as the National Association for the Education of Young Children (NAEYC) or the American Alliance for Health, Physical Education, Recreation and Dance (AAHPERD).
- Parent-teacher conferences: A well-planned conference is an excellent chance for you to share your concern for an individual student with, for example, a weight problem.
- Parent resource corner: This dedicated area would provide parents and teachers with resources and educational materials, including CDs, software, cookbooks, DVDs, activity books, and magazines, related to several health topics.

Parent Participation

Parents can give added support during the school day, which teachers often need. Try the following:

- Parent aides: Parents can help in leading exercise routines, game activities, or yoga classes.
- Volunteers or monitors: Parents can assist in playground supervision or help manage and organize children while they are active.
- Facilities and equipment: Handy parents can be enlisted to help build or repair physical activity equipment, especially around the playground.
- School governance: Parents can be enlisted to serve on a wellness committee to help establish or modify school health policies, help plan school events, and so on. The committee could review important decisions related to physical activity opportunities for children and the type of school lunches served.

Home-Based Activities

The newsletter described earlier is an effective means for suggesting certain home-based activities.

- Family games: Several family games and activities are described in chapter 4 that will help renew family bonds and develop support for a healthy lifestyle.
- Family contracts: As a unit, the family agrees to exercise or undertake a physical activity together on specific days of the week (see page 61).

- Homework helpers: These fun and exciting paper-and-pencil activities will help parents educate their children about health concepts.
- Summer activity suggestions: Teachers and parents work together to develop a packet of simple ideas to help children maintain healthy activity levels and eating habits throughout the summer.

School

The Pre-K center or elementary school can serve as a primary vehicle for transmitting health-related knowledge and encouraging health-conscious attitudes and behaviors. The first step is to establish a school wellness committee. The committee might consist of a parent, teacher, school nurse, community member, grandparent, physical educator, and the food service director. With the approval of the Pre-K director or school principal, this committee could help coordinate a schoolwide effort to create a healthy school environment. Some possible roles for the team members include the following:

- Classroom teachers: Classroom teachers can serve as excellent role models for children's health. Teachers are primarily responsible for integrating the curriculum, and they may also plan daily physical activity opportunities. Curriculum integration includes infusing health content into subject-matter areas such as reading, math, and science. Classroom teachers may also plan and schedule intermittent 10- to 15-minute activity sessions several times throughout the day. Numerous classroom and other indoor activities are described throughout this book.
- Physical education: Each child should receive a well-balanced program of physical education, including rhythm, dance, games, expressive movement, play, exercise, and skills. If your center does not have a qualified physical educator, the wellness committee may be enlisted to help identify personnel to lead in this area. You could contact the local university for potential students qualified to assume this role on a part-time basis.
- School food service: The school's food service is an ideal way to establish healthy eating patterns in children. Considerations for breakfast, lunch, snacks, and school parties should be reviewed by the wellness committee. Efforts should be made to reduce the fat, sodium, and sugar in the foods provided through the school.
- Special services: The school nurse, psychologist, social worker, speech specialist, and music teacher all bring a special perspective on children's health. For example, the music teacher can help teach children active folk dances. Special services personnel can be a big help when organizing a health fair, conferencing with parents, or providing their insights into a child's special needs and interests.

Some preschools offer exercise equipment designed specifically for children.

Photo courtesy of Sport-Fun.

Community

Although the contributions of the home and school are critical to a child's health, the role of the community should not be underestimated. To work effectively with the community, conduct a survey of the demographics as well as existing community structures, including civic groups, businesses, and recreation centers, to learn more about the potential opportunities for children to participate in physical activity. This survey will also be a positive step in building community relationships throughout the year.

Include one or two community members on the school's wellness committee, such as a member of the Chamber of Commerce or a board member of the local senior citizens organization. This initial outreach will help establish a positive relationship with the community.

Here are a few suggestions for reaching out to the community:

- Take field trips to local restaurants, medical facilities, parks, and so on.
- Communicate your school's new health initiative through the local newspaper.

- Develop a relationship with several businesses. They may donate goods and services to your school. Perhaps a yogurt store will offer "buy one, get one free" certificates that you can distribute to children as incentives.
- Take a small group of children on a field trip to another preschool. Arrange play activities and a snack.
- Offer your school as a site for civic meetings, evening fitness classes, or youth sport activities for the community.
- Give presentations to local groups such as senior citizens. They, in turn, may volunteer to help at your school.
- Arrange special community projects such as cleanup and beautification of the school grounds and the surrounding neighborhood.

The community can provide the finishing touch to your efforts to create a healthy environment for young children. Your efforts will also help create stronger bonds between the school and the community that may result in additional positive outcomes.

SEVEN KEYS TO AN ACTIVE START

The preface and this chapter have explained the issues related to childhood obesity, established the premise of the book, reviewed the philosophy for creating positive health habits in young children, and described the two major action strategies: giving children an early start and using a team approach.

The following are powerful benchmarks for getting young children active as you use this resource throughout the year. Keep in mind that the "keys" to an Active Start will help open a child's world to a lifetime of physical activity.

1. Opportunity

When children are provided with ample opportunity, they choose to be more physically active. Create opportunities through the types of toys, games, and facilities children are exposed to throughout the day. Parents should plan weekly trips to the park, beach, or recreation centers. Teachers and administrators should structure school policies, schedules, and physical planning to ensure that children have an opportunity to be active.

2. Daily Dose

If we expect children to adopt a long-term habit of physical activity, the specific behavior must be practiced. Children should be physically active every day through a variety of physical activities. Follow the Active Start guidelines (chapter 2). Plan for at least 60 minutes of **structured physical activity** and 60 minutes of **unstructured physical activity** time every day. Preschool teachers and parents should agree on a simple model for scheduling a minimum total physical activity time, such as 90 minutes at school and about 30 minutes at home during the week.

3. New Motor Skills

Motor skills serve as a foundation for physical activity in young children. When children explore and acquire age-appropriate movement skills (skipping, hopping, jumping, catching, throwing, and so on), they become and tend to remain physically active for many years. Expose children to a wide variety of skills using an array of equipment such as beanbags, hoops, play balls, **parachutes,** scarves, and the like. Pay more attention to the way children are performing the skills than to how successful they are at using the skills (for example, scoring a goal or striking a ball for distance).

4. Individual Choice

Allow children to make choices in the area of physical activity. If you provide children with a variety of experiences, they will show you what they enjoy. Use that as a springboard to enhancing their physical activity. Also, don't limit children to a specific dose of physical activity (e.g., "Everyone run up and around the maple tree" or "Everyone try five jumping jacks"). Allow children to develop their own personal preferences. Some may feel more comfortable *walking* up and around the maple tree or doing *eight* jumping jacks instead of the five you requested. When children are allowed to make choices, they feel more empowered in the physical activity environment.

5. Role Models

Children will become socialized much earlier in life when the people they value most—parents, caregivers, teachers, grandparents, siblings, and friends—are positive role models. Children love to imitate actions and behaviors of the people they respect. Remember the old adage: "Actions speak louder than words."

6. Noncompetitive Activity

Select activities that are fun and enjoyable rather than those that pit one student against another. If children are exposed to a high percentage of competitive activity at ages two through six, they will come to believe that competition is the most important reason for learning new skills and engaging in physical activity. As discussed earlier, competition in sport is developmentally inappropriate between two and six years of age for several reasons.

Some games and activities described in this book are mildly competitive; however, winning and losing are not emphasized, and teachers and parents are encouraged to promote enjoyment of the activity rather than whether one group performed a little better than another. Children should be consistently reminded that the important thing is to do their "physical best." A good mantra to use is "If you had fun, you won!"

7. Family Affair

Caregivers, teachers, grandparents, and friends are important role models for children, but the most powerful influence is the child's home environment. In fact, the same-sex gender influence is especially important. For example, boys are more tuned in to how dad spends his time, how he dresses, how he speaks to others, and so on. Parents and stepparents who include young children in family activities such as hiking, skating, swimming, fishing, and biking will be sending their children a powerful message about the value of physical activity. Also, how the parents view the role of food, as well as the types of food eaten in the home, will have a significant impact on a child's values about food consumption and weight control (see chapter 3 for specific guidelines).

SUMMARY

Childhood obesity has evolved into a critical global problem. Parents, teachers, politicians, and community members throughout the world can no longer sit on the sidelines—they must take action.

Begin by establishing the principles that will guide your philosophy. Implement this philosophy at an early age to establish positive health behaviors. But don't go it alone. Incorporate a team approach in which the home, school, and community are equally involved in developing a child's health habits. Finally, try to use the seven keys to an Active Start throughout the year as benchmarks for selecting developmentally appropriate physical activity for young children.

The answer lies not only in getting children active but also in establishing a long-term pattern for a healthy lifestyle. By incorporating the philosophy and principles outlined in this chapter, you will be off to a great start—an Active Start!

© Corbis

BUILDING A FOUNDATION

Do you find yourself using the same old games and activities, year in and year out, with children ages two through six—Duck, Duck, Goose, Simon Says, and various tag games such as freeze tag? How about the same old snacks, drinks, and meals—peanut butter and jelly sandwiches, cookies and milk, peanut butter on a cracker, fruit punch, and soda? Many of these so-called common practices and traditions handed down from one generation to the next are in need of change. Perhaps these traditions that have perpetuated throughout the world for many years are partially to blame for the obesity levels in children today.

This chapter will outline the possibilities for change by providing a new **physical activity** pyramid for young children and reviewing the national Food Guide Pyramid for Young Children ages two through six. The chapter will also provide developmentally appropriate practices for movement programs as well as the Active Start physical activity guidelines for children birth through five years of age. The content outlined will serve as a foundation for initiating changes in the physical activity and eating patterns of young children.

THE PHYSICALLY EDUCATED PERSON

The primary goal of any parent, teacher, or caregiver is to educate the total child. Attention should be directed at the mental, social, emotional, and physical makeup of each child. This holistic approach has been enhanced by the National Association for Sport and Physical Education (NASPE). In 1992, NASPE developed a document titled *The Physically Educated Person*, which can also serve as a guideline for children ages two through six. It states: *A physically educated person*

- *has learned skills necessary to perform a variety of physical activity.* Children ages two through six are developing or acquiring skills.
- *is physically fit.* Children ages two through six are developing **cardiorespiratory endurance**, **muscular endurance**, and **flexibility** and learning healthy eating habits to control weight.
- *does participate in regular physical activity* (see the Active Start guidelines on pages 22-24).
- *knows the implications of and benefits from involvement in physical education.* Children ages two through six know the rules and directions for game play; learn about body parts, muscles, bones, and how they move; know that physical activity is a healthy practice; and learn to communicate through movement and apply various **movement concepts** to skills.
- *values physical education and its contribution to a healthy lifestyle.* Youngsters appreciate physical activity as fun and enjoyable; they value the relationships with others that result from physical activity and value physical activity as a daily practice that develops a sense of self.

STRIKING A BALANCE

Both the physical activity levels and the eating habits of young children should be of primary concern to parents, teachers, and caregivers. Striking a balance at a young age with a wide variety of activities and foods will help establish healthy lifestyle patterns. Specific planning and monitoring are necessary to ensure that children are getting the proper quality and quantity of physical activity and nutrients (see figure 2.1).

The Active Start Pyramid for Young Children outlines a balanced approach to a child's physical activity patterns. For more specific recommendations related to time segments and frequency, refer to the Active Start guidelines on pages 22-24.

The USDA MyPyramid (2005) includes recommendations for a healthy diet based on age, gender, and activity levels.

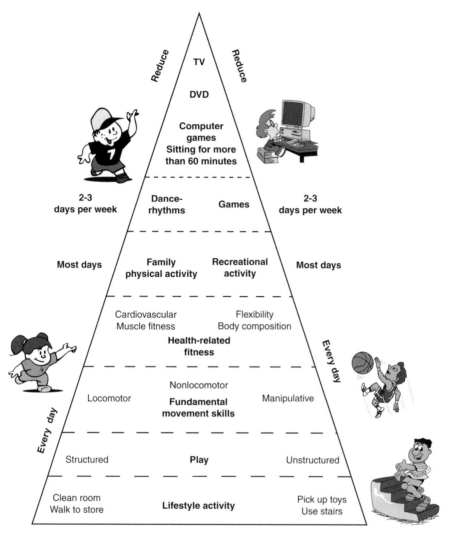

Figure 2.1—The Active Start Pyramid for Young Children, ages two to six.

Lifestyle Activity

This section of the pyramid is important for establishing basic physical activity patterns. Children need some structure in their lives; their daily routines can include activities such as cleaning their room, picking up toys, walking or playing with pets, backyard **play,** helping around the house, gardening, walking, and using the stairs instead of riding in vehicles or elevators. Lifestyle activity should be planned every day.

Play

Play is a young child's world. It is the way children physically explore their environment, develop language and social skills, and enhance their imagination and creativity. Children participate in two types of play: structured and unstructured.

Structured play is planned and directed by a parent, teacher, or caregiver for a specific amount of time (for example, a "circle time" game or dance). Unstructured play is child-initiated play that develops from a child's imagination or interests. Adults should help create opportunities for unstructured play throughout the child's day. An example would be children creating a new activity on the playground climbing equipment. Unstructured play may be an individual or small-group activity. Children should have time to play every day.

Fundamental Movement Skills

Fundamental movement skills are essential to the physical activity levels of children as they move throughout childhood. A skillful child will be more active and will continue to learn new and more advanced skills later in elementary and middle school. Conversely, children who are not skillful movers are at greater risk for becoming sedentary. Fundamental movement skills should be enhanced through both structured and unstructured approaches. Movement skills can be classified as follows:

- **Locomotor skills** are large-muscle activities involving a change of direction of the total body. These skills include walking, hopping, skipping, jumping, gliding, sliding, leaping, galloping, and chasing.
- **Nonlocomotor skills** are various movements of the body performed from a stationary base. These skills include bending, turning, twisting, swaying, pushing, pulling, stretching, rolling, and balancing.
- **Manipulative skills** are motor skills in which the objective is to control one or more objects with the hands or feet. These skills include catching, throwing, striking, kicking, volleying, and trapping.

A variety of skills should be incorporated into a child's play every day.

Health-Related Physical Fitness

For children to experience the optimal benefits of physical activity, it must include the components of **health-related physical fitness** (HRPF): cardiorespiratory endurance, **muscular fitness**, flexibility, and **body composition**. These components of fitness represent the best opportunity for controlling disease and maintaining a healthy weight throughout life. Children should participate in at least two components of HRPF every day under the supervision of a parent, teacher, or caregiver.

Cardiorespiratory Endurance

Cardiorespiratory endurance (CRE) is the capacity of the heart, blood vessels, and lungs to deliver nutrients and oxygen to the tissues and remove waste products, thereby providing the energy necessary for endurance activities. Running, biking, swimming, and skating are all examples of CRE activities, and they all do one very important task—they increase the amount of oxygen the heart pumps to the working muscles.

Children between the ages of two and six are intermittent movers. Plan for short segments of CRE or any large-muscle activity such as a locomotor skill with brief rest periods in between. This approach, often called "interval activity," is an excellent way to develop a child's cardiorespiratory system and enhance physical activity levels throughout the day.

Muscular Fitness

Muscular strength is the capacity of a muscle or muscle group to exert maximum force against resistance. Strength exercises using maximum resistance are unsafe and not recommended for children ages two through six.

Muscular endurance is the capacity of a muscle or muscle group to exert force over a period of time against a resistance that is less than the maximum one can move. This type of resistance exercise is recommended for children performing under adult supervision and using proper form and technique. Children can use rubber resistance bands, walk across the playground horizontal ladder, climb monkey bars, or perform a modified curl-up, often referred to as a sit-up. All are examples of muscular fitness activities.

The general benefits of muscular fitness activities for children include the following:

- Performing lifestyle activities—picking up toys, cleaning their room, opening doors, drawers, and closets.

- Good posture support. Strong muscles help keep a child's neck and back properly aligned.
- Joint support. Strong muscles reduce the stress on major joints, especially the knees, shoulders, and hips. Resistance exercise will also help build bone density during childhood, a critical time of development.
- Protection of internal organs. Strong abdominal muscles help keep the internal organs intact. Well-developed shoulder, back, and chest muscles promote heart and lung efficiency.
- Improved muscular strength. Strong muscles translate into more time spent on activity such as skills, games, rhythms, and dance. Children will not fatigue as fast and will enjoy the activity for longer time periods. Resistance exercise will also protect the major joints and soft tissue from stress and injury as a result of repeated movements such as kicking.

© Human Kinetics

Catching a ball is a fundamental movement skill.

Flexibility

Flexibility is the ability to move the joints in an unrestricted manner through a full range of motion. Young children generally have flexible muscles, ligaments, and tendons but should be encouraged to stretch on a daily basis. Also, children who maintain an active lifestyle in a wide variety of activities will enhance flexibility. Be sure to include several minutes of **static stretching** after an activity.

Static stretching consists of slowly and steadily stretching a muscle group to a hold or stable position. Try to prevent children from making bouncing or jerking movements when stretching, often called **ballistic stretching**, which could eventually damage the muscles and joints.

The benefits of flexibility are preventing injury, reducing muscle soreness, maintaining posture, reducing stress on joints, and improving skill performance.

Body Composition

Body composition is the ratio of body fat to lean body tissue (e.g., muscle, bone, and internal organs). All children need body fat for proper liver function and brain development; however, too much fat can lead to obesity and other serious health problems. Although increasing physical activity levels is a critical factor in controlling body fat, a quality nutrition education program is equally important in maintaining a healthy body weight (see the USDA MyPyramid on page 16).

Family Physical Activity

The family unit has a significant impact on the habits and behaviors of young children. Parents have a responsibility for planning family activities most days of the week or at least four times per week. Simple activities such as a day at the beach, playground visits, or playing catch as a family should be consistent occurrences throughout the week. Parents and older siblings can serve as excellent role models for younger children. Brothers, sisters, grandparents, and caregivers might help fill in for busy parents. See chapter 4 for guidelines, suggestions, and several active family fun ideas.

Recreational Activity

Children should also view physical activity as a positive use of leisure time, rather than watching TV or sitting in front of a computer screen. Expose children to activities such as camping and fishing, biking, playing with friends, hopscotch, backyard toys, or ice skating. Enroll children in a local yoga program for kids or dance classes in your community, take them to the pool for open swimming, or take a walk to the library. Encourage children to participate in recreational activity at least four times a week.

Rhythms and Dance

Children enjoy moving to music. The combination of rhythms and physical activity can be a motivating, uplifting experience. Try to incorporate structured time for this type of movement at least two days per week (see chapter 8).

Games

Games of low organization (indoor or outdoor) are helpful when working with more than three children at a time. Games of low organization are simple activities with one or two rules and minimal game strategies. These games often include one or more basic motor skills. Be sure a game is developmentally appropriate and that competition between groups of children is not emphasized. This could be a positive way to keep youngsters motivated and moving at least two days per week.

In summary, look for ways to reduce the time children spend watching TV, playing video games, or sitting for more than 60 minutes at a time. Try to include more activity time if they are too sedentary. Children should be up and moving every 60 minutes throughout the day to satisfy their need for intermittent activity. Schedule and monitor time for TV, video games, and the computer, but limit the time spent in these activities if it is at the expense of more physical activity.

MyPyramid Plan

In childhood, early food experiences are critical to the formation of lifelong food preferences and habits. Children ages two through six have special nutrition needs and eating patterns compared to older children and adults. To help improve the eating behaviors of children and adults ages two and up, the USDA has developed the MyPyramid (see figure 2.2).

The pyramid was developed based on the USDA document *Dietary Guidelines for Americans* (2005). The dietary guidelines describe a healthy diet as one that emphasizes fruits, vegetables, whole grains, and fat-free milk products. It includes lean meats, poultry, fish, beans, nuts, and foods low in saturated fats, trans fat, cholesterol, salt, and added sugars. For the complete 70-page document, see www.health.gov/dietaryguidelines/dga2005/document.

The MyPyramid is personalized. Simply visit www.mypyramid.gov and type in your child's age, gender, and activity level in the fields provided. The following is an example of a four-year-old male child who is physically active more than 60 minutes a day.

MyPyramid.gov
STEPS TO A HEALTHIER you

Figure 2.2—MyPyramid.
U.S. Department of Agriculture.

Sample MyPyramid Plan

Based on the information you provided and the average needs for your age, gender, and physical activity (Age: 4, Sex: male, Physical Activity: More than 60 minutes) your results indicate that you should eat these amounts from the following food groups daily.
 Your results are based on a 1600 calorie pattern.

 Grains: 5 ounces (142 grams)
 Vegetables: 2 cups (450 grams)
 Fruits: 1.5 cups (340 grams)
 Milk: 3 cups (710 milliliters)
 Meat and beans: 5 ounces (142 grams)

General tips are offered in each food group:

Grain Group

 bread (whole-wheat or whole-grain bread)
 cooked rice (preferably brown rice)
 ready-to-eat cereal (low fat, low sugar)

(continued)

21

Sample MyPyramid Plan (continued)

— Vegetable Group

chopped raw (clean thoroughly) or cooked dark green and orange vegetables (do not overcook)

— Fruit Group

fresh fruit such as strawberries, blueberries, and melon
juice (natural, unsweetened)
dried fruit (figs, plums; cut into small pieces)

— Milk Group

milk (nonfat milk, soy milk, or rice milk) or yogurt
cheese (low fat)

— Meat Group

cooked lean meat, poultry, or fish (trim fat from meat; serve skinless chicken, fresh fish [salmon, cod, halibut])
cooked dry beans (black beans, lima beans)
peanut butter

— Fats and Oils

Crackers, cookies, sweets (select choices low in saturated fat and products containing no partially hydrogenated oils)

Vary the types of food served, as it will take time for children to acquire tastes for certain foods. Also, allow children to select foods and determine how much they want to eat at a sitting. See chapter 3 for specific guidelines and exciting food choices and recipes to meet recommendations in the MyPyramid published by the USDA (2005).

ACTIVE START
A Statement of Physical Activity Guidelines for Children Birth to Five Years

The motivation for this book came from my work as a coauthor of the Active Start guidelines. Although this book focuses on ages two through six, the guidelines serve as the anchor for this resource and provide a perspective for the need to get children active from birth. The hope is that the guidelines, recommendations, and the innovative activities contained in later chapters will enable parents, teachers, and caregivers to get young children moving on a daily basis.

Over the past several years, the National Institutes of Health, the Centers for Disease Control and Prevention, the American College of Sports Medicine, and the National Association for Sport and Physical Education have developed and published physical activity guidelines for school-aged children to adults. Guidelines for young children, infants, toddlers, and preschoolers, however, were not included in these publications.

A committee was formed consisting of specialists in motor development, movement, exercise physiology, and fitness education to construct the Active Start guidelines supported by NASPE. Currently, research data on the physical activity levels for this age group are limited. The committee developed the guidelines based on well-founded theories of childhood development and the alarming biomedical research related to childhood obesity. Research strongly supports that children get progressively heavier and their physical activity levels decrease as they reach puberty, and this pattern continues into adolescence and adulthood.

All children birth to age five should engage in daily physical activity that promotes health-related fitness and movement skills. In light of the changing developmental needs of children from birth to age five, the guidelines were divided into three levels: infants, toddlers, and preschoolers. Five guidelines were developed for each group and are intended to answer questions related to the kind of physical activity suitable for infants and young children, the environment for the physical activity, and the individuals responsible for facilitating the physical activity.

Infants (Birth to 12 months)

1. Infants should interact with parents or caregivers in daily physical activities that are dedicated to promoting the exploration of their environment.
2. Infants should be placed in safe settings that facilitate physical activity and do not restrict movement for prolonged periods of time.
3. Infants' physical activity should promote the development of movement skills.
4. Infants should have an environment that meets or exceeds recommended safety standards for performing large-muscle activities.
5. Individuals responsible for the well-being of infants should be aware of the importance of physical activity and facilitate the child's movement skills.

Toddlers (12 to 36 months)

1. Toddlers should accumulate at least 30 minutes daily of structured physical activity.
2. Toddlers should engage in at least 60 minutes and up to several hours of daily, unstructured physical activity and should not be

   sedentary for more than 60 minutes at a time except when sleeping.

3. Toddlers should develop movement skills that are building blocks for more complex movement tasks.

4. Toddlers should have indoor and outdoor areas that meet or exceed recommended safety standards for performing large-muscle activities.

5. Individuals responsible for the well-being of toddlers should be aware of the importance of physical activity and facilitate the child's movement skills.

Preschoolers (3 to 5 years)

1. Preschoolers should accumulate at least 60 minutes daily of structured physical activity.

2. Preschoolers should engage in at least 60 minutes and up to several hours of daily, unstructured physical activity and should not be sedentary for more than 60 minutes at a time except when sleeping.

3. Preschoolers should develop competence in movement skills that are building blocks for more complex movement tasks.

4. Preschoolers should have indoor and outdoor areas that meet or exceed recommended safety standards for performing large-muscle activities.

5. Individuals responsible for the well-being of preschoolers should be aware of the importance of physical activity and facilitate the child's movement skills.

Reprinted from Active Start (2002), with permission from the National Association for Sport and Physical Education (NASPE), 1900 Association Drive, Reston, VA 20191, USA.

SUMMARY

If change is to occur, traditional views of children's physical activity levels and eating habits must be examined and revised. This chapter outlined the possibilities for change in these areas by presenting a new physical activity pyramid and an updated food guide pyramid called MyPyramid. Try to post both pyramids in your classroom or home as reminders for creating a balanced, healthy lifestyle. In addition, the Active Start guidelines offer specific physical activity recommendations for infants, toddlers, and preschoolers to help you gauge whether your children are getting the proper amount of physical activity each day.

Chapter 3

© K. Vey/Jump

FUEL FOR FITNESS

The influence of our modern-day American diet and our customs and cultural traditions have contributed to a generation of overweight children throughout the world. Do the following sound familiar?

- Cake, ice cream, and cola at birthday parties
- Candy and other types of sweets for Halloween treats
- Large chocolate bunnies and eggs for Easter

- Hot dogs and hamburgers at every family barbecue, ball game, or Fourth of July celebration
- Three or four types of pie at Thanksgiving dinner
- Chocolate hearts, cupcakes, and other sweets at Valentine's Day parties

We are sending mixed messages to children. We want them to be healthy, to control their weight, and to be active, yet we adults are constantly providing them with poor examples.

The major culprits are foods and beverages high in sugar, sodium, and fat. These foods and beverages are usually consumed at the expense of more healthy choices and normally raise the daily caloric intake above what a child needs. The result is gradual and steady weight gain throughout childhood.

Children are most influenced by what they see or do between the ages of two and six. The message to parents, teachers, and caregivers is—it really starts with you. You must accept responsibility for the eating behaviors of children in your care and be positive role models. This will take some work on your part.

This chapter discusses how to overcome obstacles and presents a series of guidelines to help the teacher, parent, or caregiver develop positive eating habits in young children. It also includes some healthy recipes and recommended substitutes for unhealthy foods. Finally, it describes several active games with healthy eating as the central theme.

OVERCOMING OBSTACLES

Today's fast-paced society poses two major obstacles to a successful plan for healthy eating: pop culture (visits to fast-food chains, treats at parties and holiday time) and finding the time to plan meals (hectic schedules and busy lives make it hard to offer healthy eating choices).

Overcoming Pop Culture

The pressure to fit in and keep up with what other families are doing is a part of our American social culture, which has now spread its influence to many parts of the world. Instead of keeping your children away from parties and visits to fast-food chains, teach them how to be good decision makers. For example, if you bring your child to a local restaurant with another family, order grilled chicken with a garden salad for you and your child. Explain to the child later that this was a healthy choice and will keep him feeling better. At parties, call ahead to ask the host if healthy choices will be available for your child, such as bottled water, vegetable slices, or fruit juice. Teach children that it's okay to have a slice of birthday cake, as long as they opt for healthy choices most of the time. Allowing pop culture to determine children's eating habits will likely result in unhealthy choices later in life and gradual weight gain as they reach young adulthood.

Finding the Time to Plan Meals

Teachers, parents, and caregivers must accept this responsibility on a daily basis. Children will essentially eat what adults serve them. If your schedule is frantic and you are always on the go, you are probably picking up meals from local restaurants (pizza, chicken dinners, burgers, and fries), snacking from vending machines, or buying easy-to-prepare meals to pop into the microwave. The best way to save money and control your child's weight is to *plan*. Before shopping, plan out at least five days of meals and snacks and make a list of what you will need. Include what you will pack for lunch, snacks, bottled water, treats for friends who may visit, and so on. The planning will save you time, money, and stress during the week and provide your child with a variety of readily available healthy choices.

TOP 10 EATING GUIDELINES FOR PARENTS AND TEACHERS

Refer to the MyPyramid plan in chapter 2 (page 20) for more specific information to help you encourage healthier eating patterns in the school or at home. Following are the top 10 guidelines for shaping a child's eating habits.

1. Never Place Your Child on a Diet

Restricting nutrients at a young age can affect normal growth and development. Instead, replace high-fat and high-sugar items with the more nutrient-rich foods suggested in this chapter. If your child is overweight, increase **physical activity** levels on a daily basis. This combination will begin to reverse the weight gain process in a few months. Also, never give your child weight loss or weight gain supplements; they may not be safe or appropriate for young children. They also send the wrong message to children—that weight control can be achieved simply by taking a pill every day.

2. Be a Positive Role Model

Parents, teachers, and caregivers should first look at their own eating habits. As noted earlier, children will model the behaviors of the people most important to them. If you want to make a real difference, don't just tell children how to eat healthier, show them every day.

3. Avoid Pressure Tactics

Parents, teachers, and caregivers should provide children with well-balanced, appropriately sized meals, but it should be left to the child to decide what and how much to eat. Applying too much pressure will turn a child away from the healthy food you are providing and will lead to a power struggle. Parents who insist on forcing children to eat are establishing a negative pattern that will only become more stressful each day. Allow children to select from the choices you provide. This approach will develop a child's need to eat to satisfy personal hunger rather than to please her parents.

4. "Let's *Not* Make a Deal"

Try not to fall into the trap of making a deal each time children sit down to a meal. Offering chocolate cake as a reward for eating green beans is just another form of pressure. It makes the healthy foods less valuable and the chocolate cake the real prize. This is how many children's eating habits were shaped in the past and has proven unsuccessful. When youngsters become teenagers, they realize they can have the "prize" any time, hence eating high-fat and high-sugar foods at the expense of healthy foods dominates their decision making, and weight gain inevitably follows.

5. Breakfast—Still the Most Important Meal of the Day

Sound like an old saw? It's true! Schoolchildren who eat breakfast have fewer discipline problems, fewer absences, higher grades, and more energy throughout the day (Insel et al. 2003). A good breakfast does not have to consist of what adults consider appropriate breakfast food. Children may prefer a turkey sandwich or a bowl of soup for breakfast. If that is what they want, it is much better than eating no breakfast at all.

6. Plan Five or Six Meals Per Day

Young children are not programmed for the traditional adult model of eating three large meals a day. They should eat smaller meals about every 2 1/2 hours. A meal can consist of a healthy snack such as a slice of 12-grain whole-wheat bread with low-fat peanut butter spread and an orange slice. This takes careful planning, but it will be well worth the effort. Children will be able to maintain normal energy levels throughout the day, and in turn you will be teaching them to adapt to smaller portions of foods.

7. Serve More Fruits and Veggies

Children should have at least five servings of fruits and vegetables each day. If eating a plate of carrots and apple slices is not appealing to them, you may have to get creative. How about topping cereal with blueberries, mixing the carrots and peas with the mashed potatoes, or blending a smoothie with a half banana, a few strawberries, and nonfat ice cream? The goal is to find ways to get more fruits and veggies into a child's daily diet without creating a stressful situation.

8. Keep Children Hydrated

A lack of fluids can cause problems such as muscle weakness, lack of concentration, and headaches, to name just a few. Avoid high-fructose and caffeinated drinks such as cola, tea, or imitation fruit drinks—drinking them can lead to some water loss. On average, children should consume 2 to 3 quarts (1.9 to 2.8 liters) of fluids each day. This can be accomplished by consuming nonfat milk, vegetables and fruits, bottled water, 100% fruit juices, and the like. Sport drinks are another option and contain a liquid form of carbohydrate that will not cause stomach distress during activity. Since they contain high amounts of sugar, try diluting them with about 30% water per individual serving.

If children tell you they are thirsty, they are already dehydrated. Try to give them access to fluids at all times, and encourage frequent water breaks throughout the day.

9. Allow Occasional Sweets—for the Sweet

If you completely prohibit children from eating sweets, chances are they will rebel as they get older and eat more sweets as teens. Try to include some treats in moderation throughout childhood. Teach them that sweets are okay once in a while but not on a regular basis. If you always say no to treats, you won't be successful in teaching children the concept of balance and variety in food selections.

10. Make Eating Enjoyable

Try not to get too uptight when children are eating. The strict, polite meal decorum demanded by our Puritan predecessors may not be appropriate for children in the 21st century. Children are messy and will spill their milk and mash their food, so try to keep your cool. Many two- and three-year-olds are still experimenting with food and often will touch, smell, or lick their food before consuming it. Try to make the foods more appealing. Decorate the plates with appropriate holiday themes, and use fruits and vegetables to create funny faces. For example, cut an apple in two lengthwise and use half to create a face—use a strawberry slice for the nose, raisins for the eyes, and a tangerine slice for the mouth. Give that fruit a name!

You can also make meals more interesting by including foods from different cultures. Each week, designate one day as International Day—serve Spanish, Italian, German, Irish, or Caribbean foods. This is a great way to introduce new tastes and a variety of foods to your children.

LET'S EAT!

Many of the previous guidelines will come into play in this section. The following recipes are kid friendly and have been selected as surefire ways to get children eating healthier diets. The section is broken down into three areas: healthy choices, snack attack, and on the go. Keep in mind that these recipe selections may be served throughout the day and segmented into five or six meals per day for children ages two through six (refer to the MyPyramid Food Guide in chapter 2). For more information, contact the American Dietetic Association (see appendix A).

Caution!

Recipes may include ingredients that may cause allergic reactions in some children.

To get started, refer to table 3.1 to help modify traditional recipes and lower the saturated fat, sodium, and sugar content.

Simply adhering to the chart will make a significant difference in the fat, sodium, sugar, and total calories served to young children.

Healthy Choices

The following is a sampling of potential healthy choices for children ages two through six. Meal selections and portion sizes may vary based on the child's age and nutritional needs.

Banana Oat Muffins

(makes 1 dozen muffins)

    1 1/2 cups (180 grams) whole-wheat flour

    1 teaspoon (4 grams) ground nutmeg

    1 1/2 teaspoons (6 grams) baking soda

    1/3 cup (48 grams) brown sugar

    2 large bananas, mashed

Table 3.1 Modifying Traditional Recipes

Traditional selections	Modifications
DAIRY	
Ice cream	Sorbet, nonfat ice cream, soy ice cream, yogurt
Cheese, processed hard cheeses	Low-fat and part-skim cheeses (cheddar, American, Swiss, feta, Muenster) Mix cheese with tofu in lasagna or casserole dishes
FATS AND OILS	
Butter, lard, margarine	Vegetable oil, vegetable spreads Vegetable spray for sautéing
Canned chicken broth or bouillon cubes	Salt-free chicken broth or bouillon Prepare in advance; chill and skim off hardened fat
Mayonnaise	Low-fat mayonnaise
BREADS AND PASTA	
Biscuits, croissants, egg bread	12-grain whole-wheat bread with no trans fat
Frozen tortellini, lasagna	Fresh whole-wheat pasta cooked without salt
Prepackaged pies, cookies, snack food with butter or hydrogenated fats	Homemade baked goods with vegetable oil
FRUITS	
Canned fruit packed in syrup, sweetened fruit juice or fruit drinks	Fresh fruit, 100% natural fruit juice
MEATS	
Beef	Trim all visible fat, select lean cuts of beef, drain ground meat in hot water, let sit for 15 minutes
Chicken and turkey	Remove skin, bake or barbecue
Fish, canned seafood, tuna packed in oil, fried fish	Fresh fish (baked, broiled, or grilled), tuna packed in water
Eggs	Limit yolks to three per week Replace with egg whites or egg substitutes
VEGETABLES	
Canned vegetables, canned tomato paste, sauce	Homemade tomato sauce, fresh or frozen vegetables, low-sodium products
BEVERAGES	
Whole milk, soda, fruit drinks, iced tea	Bottled water, soy milk, nonfat milk, 100% fruit juices, smoothies, fresh vegetable juice, sport drinks with 30% water added per serving

3/4 cup (175 milliliters) fat-free milk

1 egg

1 egg white

2 tablespoons (30 milliliters) soy margarine, melted

1 cup (80 grams) rolled oats

Mix the flour, nutmeg, and baking soda. In another bowl, mix the mashed bananas, milk, brown sugar, egg and egg white, and soy margarine. Add the oats. Stir in the flour mixture. Preheat the oven to 375° F (190° C) and grease the muffin tin. Fill the muffin cups two-thirds full and bake for about 30 minutes. Cool for 5 to 7 minutes and serve.

Happy, Healthy Oatmeal

(serves 4)

2 1/2 cups (600 ml) water

1 1/2 cups (120 grams) rolled oats

1 mashed banana

1 tablespoon (5 grams) wheat germ

1 cup (145 grams) blueberries

Bring the water to a boil and add the oats and wheat germ. Cook for about 5 minutes. Remove from the heat and stir in the mashed bananas, then pour into individual bowls. Top off each bowl with blueberries in the shape of a happy face.

Lion Sandwich

(serves 1)

1 slice whole-wheat bread, toasted

2 tablespoons (30 milliliters) unsweetened applesauce

shredded coconut

banana slices

raisins

Toast the bread, then spread evenly with applesauce using a butter knife. Use a banana slice for the nose, shredded coconut for the whiskers and mane, and raisins for the eyes and mouth. Try making other animal faces or use a cookie cutter to create other animal shapes.

Peanut Butter and Banana Sandwich

(serves 1)

> 2 tablespoons (32 grams) natural low-fat peanut butter
>
> 2 slices whole-wheat bread
>
> 1 banana
>
> honey

Spread the peanut butter on one slice of bread. Add the sliced banana. Drizzle a small amount of honey over the banana. Top with the other slice of bread. Cut and serve.

Egg Salad Sandwich

(serves 1-2)

> 1 hard-boiled egg, chilled
>
> 2 cooked egg whites, chilled
>
> 2 tablespoons (30 milliliters) low-fat mayonnaise
>
> 2 teaspoons (5 grams) chopped celery
>
> 2 teaspoons (5.5 grams) shredded carrots
>
> 1 to 2 slices tomato
>
> 2 to 4 slices whole-wheat bread

Peel the hard-boiled egg. Mash the hard-boiled egg and chilled egg whites with the low-fat mayonnaise. Mix in the celery and shredded carrots. Spread evenly on a slice of bread, add a tomato slice, and top with the other slice of bread. Cut and serve.

Wonderful World of Salad

(serves 6)

> 3 cups (125 grams) chopped apple
>
> 1 cup (132 grams) soy cheddar cheese chunks
>
> 1 cup (160 grams) red grapes
>
> 1/2 cup (80 grams) green grapes
>
> 1/2 cup (60 grams) chopped walnut pieces
>
> 1/2 cup (80 grams) raisins
>
> 1/3 cup (80 grams) low-fat vanilla yogurt
>
> 1 teaspoon (20 milliliters) fresh lemon juice

Mix all ingredients thoroughly in a large bowl. Refrigerate for at least 1 hour and serve.

Butterfly Salad

(serves 2)

> 1 large lettuce leaf
>
> 1 large pineapple ring
>
> 2 scoops vanilla low-fat yogurt
>
> 6 raisins
>
> 1 celery stick
>
> 2 carrot sticks

Place the lettuce leaf on a large, flat plate. Cut the pineapple ring in two and place half on each side of the lettuce leaf. Add a scoop of the yogurt to the open space in each half of the pineapple ring to create the butterfly wings. Then nestle three raisins in the yogurt on each wing. Place a 4-inch- (10-centimeter-) long celery stick down the middle between the wings to form the body. Finish by placing two carrot sticks at the top of the celery stick to form the antennae.

Carmine's Italian Meatloaf

(serves 6)

> 2 1/2 pounds (680 grams) ground turkey
>
> 1/2 cup (40 grams) chopped onion
>
> 1 clove garlic, minced
>
> 2 mushrooms, chopped
>
> 1/2 teaspoon (1.25 grams) oregano
>
> 4 slices whole-wheat bread, crumbled
>
> 1 egg
>
> 1 egg white
>
> 3/4 cup (178 milliliters) nonfat milk
>
> 2 cups (470 milliliters) (15-ounce can) tomato sauce (If you select ready-made sauce from a jar, be sure to use low-sodium, low-fat brands.)

In a large mixing bowl, combine the turkey, egg and egg white, crumbled bread, onion, mushrooms, nonfat milk, garlic, and oregano. Also, add 1/2 cup (118 milliliters) of tomato sauce for flavor. Place in an ungreased pan and shape into a loaf. Bake for 30 minutes at 350° F (175° C). Cover with the remaining tomato sauce and bake for an additional 30 minutes.

Whole-Wheat Veggie Pizza

(serves 8)

1 16-ounce (450-gram) loaf frozen whole-wheat bread dough (thawed)

3 cups (325 grams) sliced vegetables (mushrooms, zucchini, baby eggplant, carrots, small broccoli florets)

1 1/2 cups (170 grams) shredded skim mozzarella cheese

1/2 cup (75 grams) reduced-fat feta cheese

2 tablespoons (1.25 grams) snipped cilantro

1 cup (235 milliliters) low-sodium tomato sauce

Place vegetables in a steamer basket over simmering water for 2 to 4 minutes, or until crisp-tender. Drain on paper towels. For the crust, spray two 12-inch (30-centimeter) pizza pans with nonstick spray coating. Divide dough in half. In the pizza pans, pat dough to 11-inch (25-centimeter) circles and build up edges slightly. Do not let rise. Bake in a 425° F (220° C) oven for about 10 minutes, or until browned. Remove from oven and spread tomato sauce over crust to within 1/2 inch (1 centimeter) of the edges. Layer with cooked vegetables and cheeses. Sprinkle cilantro on top. Bake for an additional 10 to 15 minutes, or until bubbly. Cut into small wedges and serve.

Snack Attack

We all get the munchies. Sometimes we just get the urge to snack on something while watching a movie or visiting with friends. Children are no different. Try getting them into the habit of eating healthy snacks by modifying the ingredients and making it fun!

- Ants on a Log: Cut celery sticks into approximately 4-inch (10-centimeter) lengths. Spread low-fat peanut butter along the celery groove. Top with four or five raisins.

- Happy Face: Spread low-fat fruit yogurt evenly over a rice cake. Make a happy face using half of a cut strawberry for the nose and raisins for the eyes and mouth.

- Hummdinger: Spread 3/4 cup (175 milliliters) of hummus on a plate. (You can purchase already-prepared hummus at most grocery stores.) Serve with cut carrot sticks, celery sticks, or breadsticks.

- Nutty Nana: Peel a medium-sized banana. Spread a small scoop of peanut butter along the top portion. Sprinkle small pieces of chocolate chips and shredded coconut over the peanut butter.

Children can have healthy foods even when on the go.

- Trees in the Forest: Prepare dip using 1/4 cup (60 grams) plain nonfat yogurt, 1/4 cup (60 grams) low-fat sour cream, 2 teaspoons (30 milliliters) honey, and 2 teaspoons (10 grams) brown mustard. Mix together and pour into a serving dish. Next, place several cut carrot sticks in the dip (for the tree trunks), then position small broccoli florets on the carrot sticks to form the tree canopy. Surround the dish with additional vegetables for dipping.
- Smoothielicious: Mix 1/4 cup (60 grams) vanilla nonfat yogurt, half a banana, two or three medium strawberries, and 3/4 cup (180 milliliters) of pineapple juice. Add chopped ice and blend for 1 minute.
- Protein Power Smoothie: Mix 1 cup soy milk (235 milliliters), 1 cup (240 grams) plain nonfat yogurt, 1 teaspoon (2.5 grams) protein powder, half a banana, and 1 teaspoon (5 milliliters) honey. Add chopped ice and blend for 1 minute.

On the Go!

If you have a busy schedule of work, appointments, household chores, after-school activities, and the like, you will need some quick-fix foods. These foods are helpful when you are on the go and can't get to the kitchen to prepare a healthy choice of your own.

- Turkey sandwich: Made with 12-grain whole-wheat bread and Applegate Farms organic deli turkey breast or any fresh meat free of nitrates and low in sodium.
- Barbara's Bakery Puffins Cereal and Milk Bars: No trans fat; only 8 grams of sugar and 3 grams of fiber.
- Earth's Best Organic Crunchin' Blocks: Banana-flavored crackers with an alphabet theme; no trans fat and low in sugar.
- Frontera Foods Cuadritos: Petite tortilla chips that are a great size for children to handle; no trans fat and low in sodium. (*Warning:* Not appropriate for children under four years of age due to risk of choking.)
- Danimals Drinkable Lowfat Yogurt: Low in fat, high in protein and nutrients.
- Tube food: Flavored yogurt in a tube—cut, squeeze, and eat.
- Mediterranean TERRA Chips: Vegetable chips with no trans fat that are low in sodium; break into small pieces.
- Ultimate trail mix: Blend equal amounts of Rice Chex, Corn Chex, Cheerios, raisins, chopped peanuts and walnuts, nonfat pretzel sticks, and chocolate chips. Shake in a large bag, then make up several individual bags for quick snacks on the go. Break peanuts and walnuts into small pieces. (Recommended for five- to six-year-olds only—*chopped nuts may be a safety concern for younger children.*)
- Glenny's Low-Fat Soy Crisps: Low in carbohydrate, high in protein, no trans fat.
- Fresh fruit: Precut an apple, orange, banana, peach, or pear into slices and place in resealable plastic bags for convenience; simple and easy.

If you can't find the brands listed in this section, look for similar products that are low in sodium, sugar, and trans fat.

ACTIVE NUTRITION GAMES

The following games include nutrition education with an emphasis on physical activity. This is a great opportunity to satisfy a child's love of movement while reinforcing the need to eat healthy foods.

Food Rainbow . . . . Ages 2 to 6

⫸ Objectives

Color identification, reinforce healthy food choices, increase physical activity, improve locomotor skills

⫸ Participants

4 to 12 children

⫸ Equipment and Materials

12 cutout pictures of yellow food examples, 12 cutout pictures of red food examples, 12 cutout pictures of green food examples, four long jump ropes or string, sliced fruit for each child (apples, grapes, bananas)

⫸ Description

On one end of the play area, create a rainbow using the four jump ropes or string. Clearly label each area of the rainbow with the colors "Yellow," "Red," and "Green." Spread the cutout pictures of food examples throughout the play space.

Examples

> Yellow: squash, corn, grapefruit, okra, pineapples, bananas
>
> Red: apples, cranberries, strawberries, red peppers, red grapes, tomato sauce
>
> Green: grapes, broccoli, string beans, spinach, green apples, lettuce

At the signal, call out a color. Ask all children to run and pick up a food of that color, then run back to the rainbow and place the food anywhere in the matching color space. Then call out another color. At the end of the activity, remark on how beautiful the healthy food rainbow is. "For snack today, we'll have a sampling of red (sliced apples), yellow (sliced bananas), and green (grapes) foods. Let's eat!"

⫸ Modifications

Change the locomotor movements each time you call a new color. Have the children try skipping, hopping, or galloping like a horse.

Pyramid Match . . . . Ages 4 to 6

>>> Objectives

Increase physical activity, illustrate balanced eating habits using the Food Guide Pyramid for Young Children

>>> Participants

4 to 12 children

>>> Equipment and Materials

10 large hoops, four cones, 50 to 60 laminated cutout pictures of various food items

>>> Description

Arrange the hoops in the shape of the Food Guide Pyramid. Label each section within the pyramid and provide a sample picture for each category (for example, meats). Next, place at least four examples of food in each section of the pyramid. Spread out matching food examples about 15 yards (13.5 meters) from the pyramid.

Line up the children in three or four lines (depending on the number of children in the group) behind the cones, about 15 yards (13.5 meters) from the food examples. At the "Go" signal, the first child in each line runs to the food examples, chooses any food, and then runs to the Food Guide Pyramid. When they get to the pyramid, they have to pretend to be a "bouncing ball," jumping up and down five times to increase the physical activity of the game. Then they must match their food choice to its exact match in the pyramid by placing it in the appropriate section (for example, oranges next to oranges in the fruit section).

The children then run back to their respective lines and tag the next child in line. At the end of the game, have the entire group gather around the pyramid while you review the various sections, making any necessary corrections.

>>> Modifications

Change the locomotor movement each round (have the children skip, hop, or gallop to the pyramid).

Heart-Smart Hustle . . . . Ages 4 to 6

>>> Objectives

Increase physical activity, differentiate heart-healthy food choices, improve locomotor skills

>>> Participants

4 to 12 children

>>> Equipment and Materials

25 paper plates, 25 laminated food pictures (labeled), upbeat music, CD or tape player

>>> Description

On the bottom of each paper plate, tape a picture of a food with the appropriate healthy or unhealthy label. Spread the plates throughout an open play area with the serving side up. Have the children scatter themselves around the play area. Start the music and ask the children to first walk around the area without stepping on a plate. When the music stops, the children grab the plate closest to them, turn it over, and look at the picture. If they see a heart-healthy food, they remain standing. If they see an unhealthy food, they sit. Then, as the music begins again, the children who are standing each go to one of the seated children and free them with a tap on the shoulder, and all play on.

Healthy choices	Unhealthy choices
Skinless chicken	Fast-food hamburger
Apples	French fries
Grapes	Candy bar
Soy milk	Hot dogs
Oatmeal	Ice cream
Raisins	Pepperoni

≫ Modifications

Have the children free the seated children by both of them performing a selected physical activity (for example, five jumping jacks). Change the loco-motor skill for each round.

Hooked on Health . . . . Ages 4 to 6

>>> Objectives

Differentiate between healthy and unhealthy foods, increase physical activity

>>> Participants

8 to 12 children

>>> Equipment and Materials

Yardstick or plastic stick about 3 feet (1 meter) long for each child, string, magnets, two bags labeled "Healthy" and "Unhealthy," laminated examples of various healthy and unhealthy foods, large paper clips, 8 to 12 cones, upbeat music, CD or tape player

>>> Description

Construct a fishing rod for each child by tying a 3-foot- (1-meter-) long piece of string to one end of a yardstick or plastic stick. Attach a large paper clip to the end of the string. Attach a magnet to the laminated food examples. Create a circular pool area at the far end of the play area using 8 to 12 cones (one per child), and place a fishing rod securely in the hole of each cone. At the other end of the play area, have the children perform various locomotor skills to music. When the music stops, call out a specific movement such as skipping. After 30 seconds or so, call out "Fish on!" All children jog over to the pond, grab a fishing rod, and try to "catch" a food card by placing the paper clip on the magnet attached to the card. After reeling in the food card, the child places it in the appropriate bag ("Healthy" or "Unhealthy") located about 10 yards (9 meters) from the pond, then jogs back to "fish" for additional food items.

At the end of the activity, take the unhealthy food items from the bag and throw them back into the pond, but keep the healthy foods.

>>> Modifications

Each time the music stops and you call out the "Fish on!" signal, change the locomotor skill (for example, "Fish on! Hop to the pond").

Top 10 Terrible List

Here is my list of the top 10 worst choices for children's foods and beverages:

10. Potato chips
9. Packaged luncheon meats
8. Fast-food hamburgers
7. Candy bars
6. Ice cream or whole milk
5. Imitation fruit drinks
4. French fries
3. Doughnuts
2. Soda pop
1. Hot dogs or corn dogs

You may want to send this list home to parents with a warning label. If you are a parent, send this list to the preschool teacher or caregiver. The items were selected because of the disproportionate amounts of sodium, sugar, saturated fat, calories, and trans fat contained in the ingredients or the way the food is processed or prepared.

SUMMARY

The information in this chapter reinforces the need to establish healthy eating patterns and increase physical activity levels in young children. Many adult caregivers do not pay enough attention to the foods children are consuming on a daily basis and often send contradictory messages to children, such as giving them cake and candy for special events.

Begin by recognizing the obstacles that exist in your life and try to modify them. Refer to the mypyramid.gov Web site developed by the USDA for general guidelines on diet recommendations based on age, gender, and activity levels. Review the Top 10 Eating Guidelines for Parents and Teachers and try to incorporate one or two guidelines each week as a way of getting started. Last, gradually begin to change what foods you serve and how you prepare meals and snacks for children. Try some of the kid-proven recipes included in this chapter; they are easy to prepare, fun, and offer excellent healthy choices.

© Comstock

FUN FAMILY PHYSICAL ACTIVITY

Parents are the most influential force in a child's life. Studies have found that children are more likely to be active if their parents or siblings are active, if their parents support **play** and **physical activity**, and if they have convenient access to play areas and equipment outdoors.

Teachers can help by educating parents about the benefits of physical activity and good nutrition. They can also communicate to parents that the health of their child is a critical parental responsibility and should not be taken lightly.

Parents should be mindful of the following simple guidelines as they undertake fun family fitness activities.

1. Be a good role model. When you get up off the couch and move, your children will do the same.

2. Plan ahead. Today's hectic lives and busy schedules make it wise to plan specific times or days for the entire family to get together for fun activity.

3. Provide opportunities for physical activity. Children need convenient opportunities to be active. Take frequent trips to the beach, park, playground, active amusement parks such as water rides, snow-sledding hills, and so on.

4. Enroll children in local classes. Check with local community organizations (YMCA, Jewish Community of Centers [JCC]), colleges, and universities for programs such as yoga for kids, dance, swimming, and tumbling for tots, and visit at least two classes before you enroll. This will show your child that you place a high value on physical activity.

5. Select noncompetitive activities. Select activities where there is no winner or loser, especially between siblings. Try to convey the message that enjoyment of the activity is more important than competition.

6. Make activity part of special events. Play active games at parties and holiday get-togethers or incorporate a trip to the local park for exercise. Purchase birthday and holiday gifts that promote activity, such as tricycles, play balls, or **hoppity hops**. Select Halloween costumes that depict action, such as a basketball player or fireman.

7. Choose activities that are fun. Use popular music and animated characters that children recognize and are motivated by to inject additional excitement into your physical activity time.

The fun physical activities described in this chapter are designed for parents to share with their children. However, many of the activities can be adapted for use in the preschool setting. For example, activities such as Backyard Bubbles, Zoo Wild, and the Bubble-Wrap Broad Jump could be performed indoors on a mat, and the Squirrels Squirreling obstacle course could be set up on a large mat or carpeted surface as well.

The Snake in the Grass, Circle Shoe Jump, and Sponge Toss activities could be done in an outdoor area as long as the weather permits and there is adequate supervision. The latter would probably require the children to wear some type of waterproof garment to keep their clothing from getting too wet and may therefore be inappropriate for a school setting.

The Exercise Easter Egg Hunt, Sidewalk Scavenger Hunt, A to Z of Mall Walking, NBA (National Baby Association) Basketball, and Get Up and Pick Up activities could be adapted for the preschool setting with little modification.

Remember, when planning indoor games and activities, always make safety a priority. Establish boundaries, and make sure the play area is clear of obstacles and hazards.

Splish Splash . . . . Ages 2 to 3

≫ Objectives

Identify body parts, teach good hygiene

≫ Participants

One child

≫ Equipment and Materials

Bathtub, towel, washcloth, soap, the song "Splish Splash" (original recording by Bobby Darin or the kids' version on "The Best of Elmo from Sesame Street" CD), CD or tape player

≫ Description

Bath time can be a stressful time of the day, but not if you make it fun! Before putting your child in the tub, play the song "Splish Splash" and ask her to move different body parts to the beat of the music—arms, legs, hands, waist. Continue to play the song as you place the child in the tub. Hand the child a soapy washcloth and ask her to wash different body parts as you call them out—face, legs, toes, elbows. You may have to help younger children.

≫ Modifications

Hold up pictures of various body parts and see if your child can point to the matching part on her body.

››› *Objectives*

Creative expressive movement

››› *Participants*

2 to 12 children

››› *Equipment and Materials*

12 pictures of animals, index cards, tape, a large bag, jungle music, and CD or tape player (optional)

››› *Description*

Together with the children, find pictures of zoo animals in books and magazines. Photocopy the pictures or cut them out and tape them to index cards. Place the index cards in a paper bag. Then ask each child to select an index card (No peeking!) and act out the animal's movements for 10 to 15 seconds.

Roaring, growling, hissing, and hooting are encouraged! The other children must guess what animal is being imitated. Then have all the children imitate that animal. Continue playing until each child has had a chance to select a card and imitate the animal.

››› *Modifications*

Play jungle music during the activity to make it more exciting.

NBA (National Baby Association) Basketball . . . . Ages 2 to 3

»» Objectives

Underhand tossing skills

»» Participants

One child with parent

»» Equipment and Materials

One round plastic laundry basket, one piece of cardboard, one pair of scissors, masking tape, one lightweight plastic ball with a 6-inch (15-centimeter) circumference

»» Description

Cut a hole in the bottom of the laundry basket large enough for the ball to pass through. Use the cardboard to form a U-shaped return platform and attach it under the hole in the bottom of the basket. Set the basket 3 to 4 inches (7 to 10 centimeters) off the floor on a bottom support so that it tilts slightly forward.

Have the child sit or stand 3 to 6 feet (1 to 2 meters) from the basket and toss the ball underhand using two hands. When the ball goes through the hole in the basket, it will return to the child.

»» Modifications

Older children (ages four to six) can stand 7 to 8 feet (2 to 2.5 meters) away and try to bounce the ball once before making a basket.

Sidewalk Scavenger Hunt . . . . Ages 2 to 3

>>> *Objectives*

Increase physical activity levels, walking skills, counting skills

>>> *Participants*

Parents, two or three children

>>> *Equipment and Materials*

One lightweight plastic basket

>>> *Description*

Plan this activity on a pleasant day. Explain to the children that you are going on a scavenger hunt throughout the neighborhood. Before you begin, review the items you will try to find and how many of each:

> Two rocks
>
> Three twigs
>
> Three pebbles
>
> Four blades of grass
>
> One weed
>
> One flower

Walk together throughout the neighborhood as a family, taking care to stay on the sidewalk. You will have to help the children find and count the items on the scavenger hunt list. When all the items have been found, head back home and help the children review the list and count the number of items found.

>>> *Modifications*

Go to the beach or the local park and add different items to the scavenger hunt.

Squirrels Squirreling .... Ages 2 to 3

>>> Objectives

Crawling skills; **movement concepts**—over, under, through, in, and out

>>> Participants

One to two children

>>> Equipment and Materials

One large open-ended box, a table, four large pillows, one foam noodle, several sheets and blankets, two chairs, crepe paper, tape, toys

>>> Description

Together with your child, set up the obstacle course described below in your family room. Fashion a squirrel's tail out of crepe paper, curling it and cutting small slices at the end of the tail for style. Tuck the tail into the back of each child's pants, allowing about a 12-inch (30-centimeter) length to hang out.

Explain to the children that they will make believe they are squirrels taking food (nuts and acorns) back to their nest. Use several safe children's toys and pretend they are nuts and acorns. Only one piece of food can be taken to the nest at a time. Show the children the pathway they must take and the order in which they must go around the obstacles in your family room.

1. Through the large box
2. Under the blanket (tape the blanket edges on each side)
3. Under the bench (two chairs with a foam noodle across the seats)
4. Over the large pillows (couch cushions)
5. Under the table
6. Into the squirrel's nest (construct a cavelike setting by draping sheets over chairs or couches)

Have the children make several trips until they have collected all the acorns. Then try to crawl into the cave with the children and keep them warm, just as the squirrels do when winter arrives in cold climates.

>>> Modifications

Try this activity outdoors and use patio furniture, playground equipment, plastic tablecloths, shrubs, and bushes to design your course.

Backyard Bubbles . . . . Ages 2 to 6

>>> Objectives

Body awareness, visual tracking skills, body part identification

>>> Participants

Two to four children

>>> Equipment and Materials

Backyard or open grassy area, jar of bubble solution, table fan, plastic wand or electric bubble blower, one or two bath towels

>>> Description

Start by asking the children to burst the bubbles before they reach the ground.

Next, see how many they can catch and hold for a few seconds before they burst or hit the ground.

Then ask them to burst the bubbles again, but this time without using their hands. Instead, they must use various body parts such as their nose, elbow, knee, or toes.

Finally, have a child grab one end of a bath towel while you (or another child) grab the other end, and together try to catch as many bubbles as possible.

≫ *Modifications*

Purchase extra-strength bubble solution and try to stack the bubbles one on top of the other using an open-hole bubble catcher, or try using a piece of paper or a Ping-Pong paddle to catch and stack the bubbles.

TV Time-Out . . . . Ages 2 to 6

>>> Objectives

Increase physical activity levels during TV viewing

>>> Participants

Entire family

>>> Equipment and Materials

TV with a clear space in front of it

>>> Description

Select a favorite show the entire family enjoys watching after dinner. Each time a commercial is aired, designate a different family member to lead a different exercise.

For example, Dad goes first and says, "Everyone do 10 jumping jacks." Mom goes next and says, "Everyone march in place for 1 minute." The next family member says, "Everyone hop in place like a bouncing ball."

Keep the rotation going throughout the show; about 1 to 2 minutes of exercise is sufficient during each commercial break.

At the end of the show, each family member does their favorite stretch.

>>> Modifications

Suggest different exercises using various pieces of equipment to make the activity more interesting (for example, tossing scarves or plastic balls, or placing a rope on the floor and hopping back and forth over it).

Exercise Easter Egg Hunt . . . . Ages 2 to 6

›› Objectives

Increase physical activity levels through a traditional family activity

›› Participants

Two to five children

›› Equipment and Materials

12 to 24 dyed hard-boiled eggs

›› Description

Hide the Easter eggs throughout your backyard or at a local park. Instruct the children to place their baskets in the center of the play area, wait for the signal to "Go," then jog around the area without their baskets hunting for eggs. When they find an egg, they must hop like a rabbit back to their basket to deposit the egg. Only one egg can be carried to the basket at a time.

›› Modifications

Change the animal movements to leaping like a frog, galloping like a horse, or flying like a bird.

Wave Runner . . . . Ages 2 to 6

>>> Objectives

Increase physical activity, fleeing skills, agility

>>> Participants

One to two children with parent

>>> Equipment and Materials

Beach area

>>> Description

Begin by walking along the shoreline of the beach while holding hands with your children. As you walk along the beach, try to tiptoe away from and avoid the water as the waves wash on shore.

Next, try jogging along the shoreline with your children, this time without holding hands. Everyone is on their own—don't let the water touch your feet! Always keep your children in direct view, and stay within 5 feet (1.5 meters) of them along the shoreline.

>>> Modifications

Try challenging the waves by moving toward the shoreline when the wave rushes out, then moving quickly back up the beach when the wave rushes in.

Evening's End . . . . Ages 2 to 6

››› *Objectives*

Increase physical activity levels, family bonding

››› *Participants*

All family members

››› *Equipment and Materials*

CD or tape and CD or tape player; or exercise videos, TV, and VCR

››› *Description*

This activity will help alleviate the typical weekday blahs.

Get the family together and select two evenings during the week when all or most of you can meet. Decide on a time and note it on the family calendar located on the refrigerator. On those evenings, you all meet at the designated time for a 15-minute exercise session. Each time you meet, a different family member gets to select the music and lead the exercises. To keep the children interested, ask them what exercises they would like to do.

You should lead the first session to help get the activity off to a good start. Limit the exercise sessions to 15 minutes to help everyone stay on their personal schedules.

››› *Modifications*

Use adult or children's exercise videos to help motivate family members. Visit your local video store and ask the store manager for recommendations.

>>> Objectives

Tossing skills, accuracy

>>> Participants

Two or three children and family

>>> Equipment and Materials

One plastic bucket; three sponges—small, medium, and large sizes; tepid water; two towels; household string or cord 5 to 6 feet (1.5 to 2 meters) in length

>>> Description

Fill the bucket with tepid water to about 3 to 4 inches (7 to 10 centimeters) from the brim.

First, wet the sponges and play catch with the children using the three different-sized sponges. Wet sponges are easy for children to grasp, but you may have to cut the sponges to a size they can handle easily. Children enjoy getting splashed, so this activity is right up their alley.

Next, mark a spot about 5 feet (1.5 meters) from the bucket using the household string or cord. Have the children take turns tossing the wet sponge into the bucket. If they are having trouble, move the line closer. After a few turns, move the line back about 1 to 2 feet (30 to 60 centimeters).

Finally, teach the children that taking turns is important to active play by taking three tosses yourself, then having each child take their turn. Continue tossing for several rounds.

>>> Modifications

Use rubber bath toys or rubber balls to add excitement to this activity.

>>> Objectives

Reduce and establish limits for TV viewing time, increase family time

>>> Participants

All family members

>>> Equipment and Materials

TV-Turnoff Organizer's Kit (optional)

This kit includes tips and techniques for organizing a TV-Turnoff Week. It's filled with fact sheets, screen-free activities, curricular suggestions, quotes from past participants, best practices from around the United States, and much more. It also includes bumper stickers and posters with such slogans as "Turn off TV, Turn on Life"; "Break Free of TV"; and "Get Up and Go."

For more information, contact:

TV-Turnoff Network

1200 29th St. NW, Lower Level #1

Washington, DC 20007

www.tvturnoff.org

800-939-6737

>>> Description

According to this program, children in the United States watch an average of 4 1/2 hours of TV a day. The goal of the program is to raise awareness of the overuse of TV viewing in our nation.

The national event is usually held for a seven-day period in mid-April. The objective is to turn off the TV completely during that period. The premise is that adults and children will be more productive and will spend more quality family time together.

As you plan this week, be sure to organize specific alternatives to keep family members on task. Use several of the activities in this chapter to make family time more productive. This would also be an excellent time for reading, coloring, baking, craft projects, and visiting friends.

At the end of the week, call a family meeting to discuss how each person felt during the week. Also discuss how the family can limit TV viewing in the future.

>>> Modifications

Develop a family strategy for limiting TV watching. Schedule your own TV-turnoff week every 3 to 4 months.

Family Physical Activity
Contract . . . . Ages 2 to 6

>>> Objectives

Increase family physical activity, family unity

>>> Participants

All family members

>>> Equipment and Materials

Large calendar, paper, markers

>>> Description

Hold a family meeting to determine what days and times you can best get together as a family. Use a signed family physical activity contract to help make plans more specific and concrete and secure a commitment from each family member to participate. Place the completed contract on the refrigerator (see page 62).

Use a calendar with boxes large enough to clearly mark the days and times you agreed to be active as a family. Post the calendar on the refrigerator as well to remind all family members of the schedule.

You can also record information from completed family fitness days on a family physical activity log (see page 63).

>>> Modifications

In larger families, it may be especially difficult to get everyone together. In this case, design a contract for smaller groups of family members.

Family
Physical Activity
Contract

*W*e, the _____ family, promise that today (date) _____ we will adopt an active lifestyle and become physically active.

We acknowledge that general physical activity is very important to the health of all family members. We promise to devote _____ minutes—Mon., Tues., Wed., Thurs., Fri., Sat., Sun. (circle at least 3 days)—toward making positive changes in our physical activity. The best time of day for us to work on this change is _____ a.m./p.m.

We will try our best to fulfill this contract and develop our family fitness goals. By fulfilling this contract we will reward ourselves with a special family outing.

Family members participating—

_____   _____

_____   _____

_____   _____

This promise was witnessed by _____

From *Active Start for Healthy Kids: Activities, Exercises, and Nutritional Tips* by Stephen J. Virgilio, 2006, Champaign, IL: Human Kinetics.

Family
Physical Activity Log

Name_____ Grade_____

Date	Physical Activity	Minutes of Activity	Time of Day	How I Felt

From *Active Start for Healthy Kids: Activities, Exercises, and Nutritional Tips* by Stephen J. Virgilio, 2006, Champaign, IL: Human Kinetics.

Bubble-Wrap Broad Jump . . . Ages 2 to 6

››› *Objectives*

Jumping and landing skills

››› *Participants*

One or two children

››› *Equipment and Materials*

Approximately 6 to 8 feet (2 to 2.5 meters) of bubble wrap, 2 to 3 feet (60 to 90 centimeters) in width; colored markers or stickers

››› *Description*

Lay down a 6- to 8-foot (2- to 2.5-meter) length of standard bubble wrap on a flat, nonskid surface. Have the children stand at one end of the bubble wrap, just off the edge. Ask children in turn to bend their knees, slightly bend their back, swing their arms, and jump as far forward as possible, landing on the wrap with both feet flat. Children love to hear the bubbles popping and will want to jump again and again.

Next, mark the child's landing spot by making a mark with a permanent marker or sticker behind the heel of the child's sneaker. Each time the children try to jump forward, mark the distance with a different-colored marker or sticker so that they can challenge their personal best.

››› *Modifications*

If you don't have bubble wrap, use a flat surface and mark the distance with chalk or colored plastic tape.

A to Z of Mall Walking . . . . . Ages 4 to 6

>>> *Objectives*

Increase physical activity levels, teach object identification using letter cues

>>> *Participants*

Two or three children

>>> *Equipment and Materials*

None

>>> *Description*

Walking in the mall can be a great physical activity when the weather does not cooperate with your plans. For added physical activity, use the stairs rather than the elevators and escalators.

 As your family enters the mall, start the A to Z game by asking everyone to identify anything they see whose name begins with the letter A. When an item beginning with that letter has been found, continue finding items for each letter of the alphabet in turn. For example:

> A could be an animal,
> B could be a bench,
> C could be a clock,
> D could be a door,
> E could be ears,
> F could be food,
> and so on.

>>> *Modifications*

Change the walking pattern by walking on your toes, walking on your heels, walking with your toes pointed outward, walking fast, walking slowly, and so on.

Snake in the Grass . . . . Ages 4 to 6

>>> Objectives

Running, chasing skills

>>> Participants

Two children

>>> Equipment and Materials

One standard plastic jump rope

>>> Description

Hold one end of the rope and begin to jog around the backyard while wiggling it behind you as if it were a snake in the grass. Instruct the children to wait for the "Go" signal and then run behind you and try to catch the snake by stepping on the end of the rope. Try reversing roles, with one of the children acting as the snake in the grass while you chase from behind.

>>> Modifications

Ask two children to try this activity without parental help. One begins as the snake and the other as the chaser. Have them reverse roles so that they both get equal time acting as snake and chaser.

Circle Shoe Jump . . . . Ages 4 to 6

≫ *Objectives*

Jumping skills, timing

≫ *Participants*

Four to six children

≫ *Equipment and Materials*

One 8-foot-long (2.5-meter) jump rope, one sneaker

≫ *Description*

Tie a sneaker to one end of the rope. Have the children form a circle. Stand in the middle holding the opposite end of the rope from the sneaker. Squat down and swing the rope around in a circle, changing hands as you turn the rope to prevent it from tangling around your body. Keep the rope at a low level, and swing it at a slow but constant tempo. Tell children to jump over the sneaker when it comes around to their position in the circle.

≫ *Modifications*

Change the direction of the rope on each round. See how many times the group of children can successfully jump the sneaker.

Get Up and Pick Up . . . . Ages 4 to 6

⋙ *Objectives*

Increase physical activity, develop personal responsibility

⋙ *Participants*

One or more children and at least one parent

⋙ *Equipment and Materials*

Children's favorite music, CD or tape player

⋙ *Description*

Try to make cleaning up clutter—picking up pillows from the floor or placing toys in the toy box—a fun fitness activity.

For this activity, each family member has to pick up or clean up 10 different things in the house. Each time a family member completes a simple task, they call out a number from 1 to 10.

Another parent, grandparent, or older sibling can help the young children keep track of the number of pick-ups. When the activity ends, everyone meets in the kitchen for a healthy snack of fruit, yogurt, or soy ice cream.

⋙ *Modifications*

Play the children's favorite upbeat music. Encourage all participants to dance and sing along with the music as they clean up.

Beach Blanketball . . . . Ages 4 to 6

>>> Objectives

Tossing and catching skills, cooperation

>>> Participants

Two parents and two children or one parent and one child

>>> Equipment and Materials

Two beach towels; one 8 1/2-inch-diameter (22-centimeter) lightweight plastic ball; colored tape, chalk, or household cord

>>> Description

Begin by making a line 8 to 10 feet (2.5 to 3 meters) long in a grassy or open area using colored tape or chalk. One parent and child hold the beach towel on one side of the line, and another parent and child hold the towel on the opposite side. Place a ball in the towel. The object is to pass the ball from one side to the other as many times as possible within the length of the center line.

See how many times you can keep the ball going without it dropping. Start again and try to break your own family record.

>>> Modifications

One parent-child team can toss the ball straight up and count how many times they can keep it up.

≫ Objectives

Dodging and fleeing skills, changing directions, cooling off with summer fun

≫ Participants

One to four children

≫ Equipment and Materials

Two or three sprinklers, two or three garden hoses (You may need a two-pronged hose adapter to attach two different hoses or hose extensions.)

≫ Description

Ask your neighbors to pitch in with sprinklers and hoses. Use a variety of sprinklers: oscillating, pulsating, and hose sprinklers. Arrange the sprinklers in an open grassy area, creating a challenging course. Now turn on the water! Ask the children to run through the course without getting too wet. After several minutes, change the sprinkler arrangement for a new challenge.

≫ Modifications

If you have an automatic in-ground sprinkler system, both you and your neighbor can turn on all zones. Have the children run through both your yard and your neighbor's and back again. Run through the backyards with your children to ensure their safety.

SUMMARY

Parents are the most influential force in their children's lives and must take primary responsibility for their children's health and well-being. However, medical professionals, teachers, and parents should work as a team—with the parent serving as the head coach.

The seven guidelines for fun family physical activities outlined in this chapter will help you start planning an active family lifestyle. Many of the practical activities presented require very little equipment or special training to implement. In fact, just planning and putting together the activities can be fun for both parents and children.

Photo courtesy of Sport-Fun

LET'S EXERCISE

A significant portion of a child's daily activity time should be spent in **play**, creative movement, and lifestyle activities. You should structure some exercise time each day, however, to be sure you are covering the following major components of **health-related physical fitness**:

- **Flexibility**
- **Muscular fitness**
- **Cardiorespiratory endurance**
- **Body composition** and nutrition education (covered in chapter 3)

For many years, parents and educators believed that children ages two through six did not need to do formal exercise. The theory was that (1) they wouldn't benefit from specific exercise until puberty, and (2) the rigid approach to exercise sessions would stifle their creativity and freedom to move.

A more contemporary view has emerged over the past several years. We now know that children can gain substantial benefit from exercising before puberty, that a wide variety of **physical activity** is important for physical development, and that specific exercises such as push-ups, curl-ups, stationary bike riding, and using bands and tubes for muscular fitness may have a positive effect on a child's physical activity habits when started early in life. Children at this age want to feel "included," so they also enjoy performing physical activities and exercises similar to those their mom, dad, and older siblings participate in from time to time.

GENERAL GUIDELINES FOR EXERCISING

Before you begin designing exercise opportunities for children, keep in mind these four general guidelines:

1. Always base exercises on a child's developmental needs. Children are not adults and should not be "trained." Avoid adult approaches such as specific workouts, scheduled exercise sessions, or measuring fitness gains. Also, equipment should be tailored to the specific developmental needs of each child.

2. Structure exercise in short segments. Children will have a more positive experience when an activity is performed in short time segments or the number of **repetitions** is limited. They should have brief rest periods between activity segments rather than exercising for long continuous stretches, which is more common in older children and adults.

3. Provide children with a wide variety of exercises and activities. Strike a balance between various types of physical activity and full-body movements rather than focusing on one component of health-related physical fitness.

4. Emphasize participation and fun, not performance. Don't push children to "do a few more repetitions" or "jog another 50 yards (50 meters)." If they want to slow down or stop, allow them to do so. In turn, children will create their own comfortable segments of physical activity time. Try to establish a positive, open environment. Use upbeat music, cartoon characters, games, and innovative equipment (such as **parachutes**, bands, and **stability balls**) to make fitness a fun time for all!

STAGES OF A PHYSICAL ACTIVITY SESSION

Whether children are dancing, learning ball-handling skills, or exercising to music, a physical activity session should follow a simple three-stage approach: **warm-up**, the **main event**, and **cool-down**.

Warm-Up

The primary purpose of the warm-up is to prepare the heart, muscles, and joints for the main event. Start with simple large-muscle movements to raise the body temperature and increase blood circulation to different parts of the body. For example, begin by having children perform moderate levels of physical activity such as march steps, giant steps, backward arm circles, or slow jogging. If you plan on doing a rhythmic activity, start with music at slow to moderate levels and gradually work toward higher levels of activity.

The warm-up period should last at least 3 to 4 minutes. It does not have to include stretching, as the children would still be stretching cold muscles after a few minutes of large muscle movements. If you elect to have them stretch in the warm-up stage, keep the exercises simple and have them hold the stretch for about 10 seconds (see "Flexibility" on page 76).

Main Event

The main event is the focus of the activity session: a game, a skill activity, a dance, or an exercise routine to music. At this stage, children should be gradually moving into a higher level of physical activity. The main event should include greater amounts of physical activity time, but remember that children are intermittent learners and will need brief rest periods throughout an activity session.

Cool-Down

Begin the cool-down by gradually lowering the level of physical activity in the main event. Keep in mind that the large muscles of the body (arms, legs) return the blood to the heart. If children stop suddenly after vigorous activity, the blood will pool, which may cause dizziness or nausea. To cool down, children should perform 3 to 4 minutes of large-muscle activity at a low level of exertion, bringing their heart rate down slowly. At this point, the muscles are warm and ready to be stretched, so several **static stretching** exercises can be performed to enhance flexibility or range of motion and help prevent muscle soreness the next day.

DEVELOPMENTAL EXERCISES

The following developmental exercises and activities serve only as examples of flexibility, muscle fitness, and cardiorespiratory endurance for children ages two to six. (See chapter 3 for nutrition education ideas.) Try to incorporate these exercises and activities into various physical activity opportunities throughout the day. It will add variety and balance to the traditional "circle time" activities, play, recess time, and organized games.

The instructions are written as you might speak them directly to children, making it easy for you to begin. Study the illustrations carefully and pay close attention to proper body alignment, form, and technique to ensure that children derive the proper benefits of each health-related fitness component: flexibility, muscular fitness, and cardiorespiratory endurance.

Flexibility

Flexibility is the ability to move the joints in an unrestricted fashion through a full range of motion. The best time to enhance flexibility is during a cool-down period following several minutes of large-muscle activity when the muscles are warm and the body temperature is elevated.

Keep in mind that flexibility is joint-specific, which simply means a child with flexible hamstrings (back of the leg) may not have the same degree of flexibility in the shoulder region. For this reason, flexibility exercises should cover a full range of muscle groups (Virgilio 1997).

The following exercises should be performed in a static stretching manner—stretching and holding the movement for about 10 seconds. This is a safer, more controlled approach. When stretching, bouncing or jerking movements—often called **ballistic stretching**—should be avoided.

. . . . **Head Drop** . . . .

neck

Instructions to children: Gently drop your head, placing your chin on the center of your chest. Try to keep your shoulders still, and don't lean forward.

neck

Instructions to children: Keep your shoulders still and look straight ahead with your chin level. Slowly turn to the left and look over your left shoulder. Turn back to the center. Now slowly turn and look over your right shoulder.

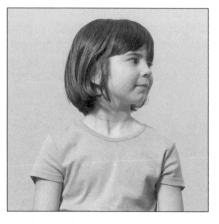

Neck Tilt

neck

Instructions to children: Slowly lower your right ear toward your right shoulder. Slowly return to the starting position. Now lower your left ear to your left shoulder and slowly return to the starting position.

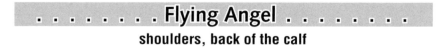

Flying Angel

shoulders, back of the calf

Instructions to children: Stand straight with your feet together and your arms at your sides. In one smooth movement, raise your arms straight over your head with the palms facing upward and, at the same time, rise up on your toes. Hold the position for a few seconds. Now slowly lower your arms to your waist and lower your heels to the floor.

Houdini Handshake

shoulders

Instructions to children: Place one hand behind your head and reach as far as you can down the middle of your back, as if you were scratching an itch. Bend your other arm around the middle of your back. Try to touch the fingers of each hand. Repeat on the other side. Whichever elbow is pointing upward, that is the shoulder you are stretching.

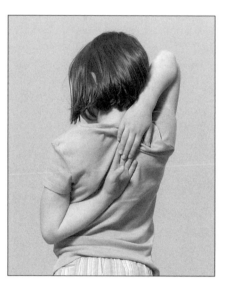

Arm Cross

shoulders, back

Instructions to children: Place your left arm across your chest while supporting your left elbow with your right hand. Use your right hand to gently pull your left arm across the front of your body (chest). Repeat on the other side.

Sit and Twist
middle back

Instructions to children: Sit with your left leg extended and the knee slightly bent. Cross your right leg over your left knee, bending your right leg. Bring your left arm across your right leg, rotating your trunk to the right side. Gently push your left elbow against your left knee. Repeat on the opposite side.

Leg Hug
lower back

Instructions to children: Lie on your back and bend your legs while grasping them under your knees. Now gently pull both knees up to your chest. Keep your lower back on the mat or carpet.

Hamstring Stretch

back of legs

Lie on your back with one foot flat on the floor and the knee bent. Pull your other knee up toward your chest. Place one hand on the calf and the other hand on the back of the thigh. Now slowly straighten that knee until you reach a comfortable position and can feel the muscles tighten. Repeat with your other leg.

Note: Never have children completely straighten or lock out the knee.

Quadriceps Stretch

front of thigh

Instructions to children: Stand upright with the top of one foot resting on a chair or platform at lower than hip height. Bend your front knee, keeping your hips and back still. Repeat with your other leg.

Note: During this stretch, have children hold onto another support for balance or hold their hand for stability.

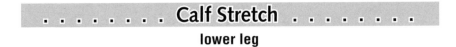

Calf Stretch

lower leg

Instructions to children: Stand facing the wall for support. Bend your front knee toward the wall. Extend your back leg straight with the foot flat on the floor and the toes pointing straight ahead. Slowly move your hips forward while keeping your back leg straight and your heel on the floor. Repeat with your other leg.

Additional flexibility movements can be found in chapter 9.

Muscular Fitness

As stated earlier, **muscular strength** and **muscular endurance** are not the same. Muscular strength is the capacity of a muscle or muscle group to exert maximum force against a resistance. Muscular endurance is the capacity of a muscle or muscle group to exert force over a period of time against a resistance that is less than maximum.

In light of their developmental level, children ages two to six should not exercise at maximum exertion levels. However, children as young as age two can do resistance exercise to enhance muscular endurance and increase strength. Therefore, this section is entitled "Muscle Fitness" to avoid confusion and provide clear direction for this health-related component of physical fitness.

Previous concerns that early resistance training adversely affected bone growth plates or produced hypertension have been discredited (Faigenbaum 2001). The opposite may be true—resistance exercise may enhance musculoskeletal development in children. Recent studies have shown that enhancing bone density in children through strength training and proper nutrition can prevent skeletal frailty in seniors.

Follow these key guidelines when developing resistance exercises and activities for children:

1. Children must be supervised at all times.
2. Resistance should be light; children should never overexert themselves to perform an exercise.
3. Never allow children to try maximum lifts where they lift the greatest weight they can in one repetition.
4. Focus on proper form and technique.
5. Machines or equipment must be appropriately sized for children. If not, the exercise may be harmful.
6. Many experts agree that one or two **sets** of five to eight repetitions is sufficient for children (Faigenbaum 2001). If children want to perform only one or two repetitions, allow them to do so and go on to another exercise.
7. Select resistance exercises that target the major muscle groups: arms, back, chest, legs, and trunk.
8. Incorporate resistance exercises on nonconsecutive days during the week.
9. Exercises should be performed slowly—one completed repetition every 3 to 4 seconds.
10. Use various approaches to make exercise fun and exciting, such as animal movements, playground equipment, resistance bands, **medicine balls,** stability balls, and parachute play.

Animal Movements

Here are some great ideas to get started. In these movements, children use their own body weight to create the resistance. For safety purposes, all animal movements should be performed on a mat.

Seal Crawl

arms, shoulders

Instructions to children: Lie on your stomach with your hands directly under your shoulders, fingers pointing slightly outward. Your feet should be 4 to 6 inches (10 to 15 centimeters) apart. Now straighten both arms, then move your hands in a right-left, right-left motion while dragging your legs along the floor. It's okay to bark like a seal as you move around the open space.

Note: If children have difficulty performing this exercise, ask them to try the seal crawl stance but not move along the floor. They can still bark.

Crab Crawl

arms, shoulders

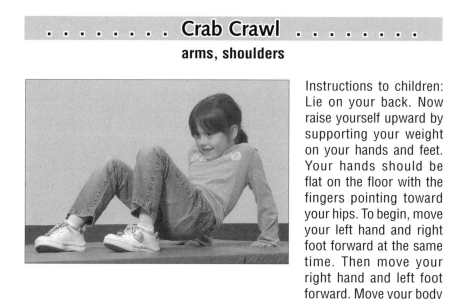

Instructions to children: Lie on your back. Now raise yourself upward by supporting your weight on your hands and feet. Your hands should be flat on the floor with the fingers pointing toward your hips. To begin, move your left hand and right foot forward at the same time. Then move your right hand and left foot forward. Move your body forward or backward.

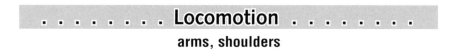

Locomotion

arms, shoulders

Instructions to children: With a partner, stand facing each other about 8 to 12 inches (20 to 30 centimeters) apart. Clasp hands, keeping your wrists firm. Begin by both of you pushing your right hand forward as your pull your left hand back. Now reverse the movement to create a locomotive. It's okay to make the locomotive "whoo-whoo" sounds, including a whistle.

Turtle Walk

arms, shoulders

Instructions to children: Lie facedown with your hands flat on the mat. Now push upward supported only by your hands and feet, with your arms straight and your knees off the mat. Keep your arms and legs wider than shoulder-width apart. Now move your right arm and leg forward together, then move your left arm and leg forward together. Try going backward.

Note: During this exercise, remind children to make small movements to reduce the stress on their joints.

Inchworm

hips, abdomen, back

Instructions to children: Sit on the floor with your arms folded across your chest and your legs extended. To move, pull your bottom and hips forward while pulling with your heels and bending your knees.

Gator Walk

arms, shoulders

Instructions to children: Lie on a mat or carpet, supporting your body with both forearms, and rise up onto your toes, keeping your back straight (gator stance). Now walk on your forearms, first with your left arm and right leg, then with the opposite arm and leg. Keep the movements small and controlled.

Note: The gator stance is a recommended lead-up to the gator walk.

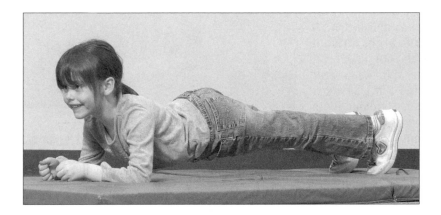

· · · · · · · · Push-Up Stance · · · · · · · ·

arms, shoulders

Instructions to children: Begin in the standard push-up position—your hands under your shoulders and your body in a straight line supported by your hands and toes, with no other parts of your body touching the ground. Hold for a few seconds.

· · · · · · · · Junior Curl-Up · · · · · · · ·

abdomen

Instructions to children: Lie on your back with your knees bent to about 140° and your feet flat on the mat. Place your arms alongside your body with the palms down. Slowly lift your head about 3 to 4 inches (7 to 10 centimeters) off the mat but continue to look straight up at the ceiling. Your hands will slide forward 1 to 2 inches (3 to 5 centimeters) along the mat. Now slowly lower your head to the mat, keeping your feet flat on the mat.

Note: Some children may be able to lift their head and shoulders off the mat during this exercise.

Treadmill

legs, abdomen

Instructions to children: Begin in a crawling position. Bring one leg up to your chest and extend the other leg backward. Begin moving by alternating your legs—right, left, right, left—in a steady rhythmic pattern. Keep your upper body still and your head level.

Wall Seat

front of legs

Instructions to children: Stand with your back flat against the wall, your feet slightly wider than shoulder-width apart, and your hands on your hips. Slowly bend your knees, sliding your back about 4 to 6 inches (10 to 15 centimeters) down the wall. Hold for a few seconds, then come back to the starting position.

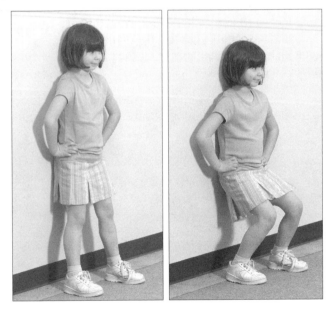

Heel Raises
calf

Instructions to children: Stand on a board or a book about 3 to 4 inches (7 to 10 centimeters) high with only your heels resting on the floor. Hold onto a chair for support and stand straight, keeping your body in line. Slowly rise up onto your toes, hold for a few seconds, then return to the starting position.

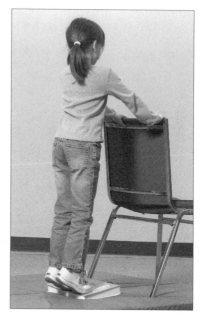

Paper Pick-Up
hand, wrist, forearms

Instructions to children: Place a clean sheet of loose-leaf paper on the desk. Try to pick up the paper and crumble it using only one hand. Now try it with the other hand.

Ball Squeeze
hand, wrist, forearms

Instructions to children: Hold a small foam-coated ball (the size of a Ping-Pong ball) in one hand. Squeeze the ball with one hand and hold for 3 seconds. Now try it with the opposite hand. Repeat several times.

Parachute Activities

The parachute is a popular piece of equipment for children. Made in various textures, sizes, and colors, it is excellent for building muscular fitness in the arms and shoulders. Through teamwork and cooperation, the entire group can exercise together and have a lot of fun doing so.

© Human Kinetics

Chute Down

arms, shoulders

Instructions to children: Everyone hold the parachute at waist level with an overhand grip, keeping your feet at least shoulder-width apart. Now everyone lift the chute overhead. At the signal, pull the chute back to your waist, using only your arms and shoulders.

Floating Cloud

arms, shoulders

Instructions to children: Everyone grasp the chute with an overhand grip. At the signal, raise the chute overhead. At the signal "Release," let go of the chute.

Wrist Rolls
wrists and forearms

Instructions to children: Everyone hold the chute straight out in front with an overhand grip. Now slowly roll the chute toward the center, keeping it tight by leaning slightly backward.

Hurricane
arms, shoulders

Instructions to children: Everyone grasp the parachute with an overhand grip. Start by making moderate (medium-sized) waves, moving the chute up and down.

Now I'll describe an approaching storm while you move the chute faster and faster in response to what is happening. "The sky is getting black, the wind is picking up, and the waves are getting larger with deep swells. Now the wind is swirling, and the waves are getting short and choppy. Oh, no, the hurricane is here!" Now move the chute up and down as fast as you can.

Note: Have the children cool down by slowing the movement of the chute as you describe how the storm is passing and everything is getting back to normal.

Superdome
arms, shoulders

Instructions to children: At the signal "Up," everyone lift the chute overhead. At the signal "Down," everyone bring the chute down to the floor. Watch the chute form a dome.

Bubble Up
arms, shoulders

This activity begins with the parachute on the floor.

Instructions to children: Everyone squat down and grasp the chute with an overhand grip. At the "Go" signal, lift the chute overhead and at the same time walk quickly into the center, forming a large bubble.

Popcorn
arms, shoulders

Start by placing several balls of various weights, sizes, and shapes in the parachute.

Instructions to children: Everyone grasp the parachute with an overhand grip. When I say "Simmer," shake the chute, creating small ripples. When I say "Cook," make the balls move more rapidly by shaking the chute harder. When I say "Popcorn," make large, fast ripples by waving your arms and jumping up and down to pop the balls straight up, but try to keep the popcorn in the pan.

Swimming Snakes

Start by placing several plastic jump ropes in the middle of the parachute. Play upbeat children's music.

Instructions to children: Hold the parachute with one hand and walk clockwise together. When the music stops, I'll yell "Swimming snakes!" All of you grip the parachute with both hands and begin moving your arms up and down to get the "snakes" (jump ropes) to start swimming. If you get touched by a snake, you have to jog around the parachute and then go back to your spot.

Note: Repeat the activity several times from the start.

Rubberized Resistance Equipment

Exercising with **rubberized resistance equipment** is a fun way to enhance muscle fitness. These lightweight, durable tubes and bands are color-coded to denote the various levels of resistance, allowing you to tailor specific exercises to individual physical needs. This equipment will not only add variety to your physical activity program but will also provide the needed resistance to various muscle groups without placing undue stress on the major joints. Exercises using resistance tubes and bands are more suited for children ages four and up.

Caution!

Never tie pieces of tubing together or allow children to play around with the tubes. Inspect the tubing for cracks each day and be certain the tubing is properly secured before performing certain exercises.

For more information about tubes and bands, visit the SPRI Products Web site (see appendix B). This company produces tubing with very light resistance levels designed especially for children ages four to six.

The following exercises are performed using three different kinds of SPRI equipment: the Xertube, QuickFit Toner tubing, and the band.

Xertube Exercises

The following exercises use the SPRI Xertube.

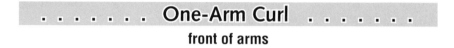

One-Arm Curl
front of arms

Instructions to children: Step on a piece of tubing and grasp one handle with your palm facing up at your side. The closer you step to the handle, the greater the resistance will be. Now curl the arm slowly toward your shoulder while keeping your elbow at your side. Repeat with your other arm.

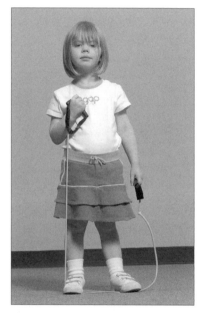

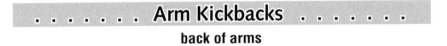

back of arms

Instructions to children: Stand in a lunge position with one foot in front of the other. Place the tubing under your front foot. Cross the tubing and grasp one handle with the hand of your nonexercising arm, then rest the arm on your upper leg. Bend forward at the waist, resting the weight of your upper body on your front leg. Grasp the other handle with your exercising arm, keeping the arm next to your hip with the palm facing backward. Keep your wrist firm and raise the arm until the palm is facing up. Return slowly to the starting position. Repeat with your opposite arm.

Upright Row

shoulders

Instructions to children: From a standing position, place both feet on the tube. Grasp the handles with both hands and position your arms in front of you, resting on your legs. Bend your elbows and pull the handles up to your chest. Slowly return to the starting position.

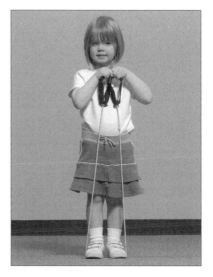

QuickFit Toner Tubing Exercises

The following exercises use the SPRI QuickFit Toner tubing.

Chest Press

chest, back of arms

Instructions to children: Stand with your feet about shoulder-width apart and your knees slightly bent. Position the toner behind your back with the padding squarely in the middle. Grasp the handles with your palms facing outward. Extend your arms forward, keeping a slight bend in the elbows. Return to the starting position.

arms, shoulders

Instructions to children: Grasp the toner with one arm straight out in front of you, as if you were holding a bow at shoulder height. With your other hand, draw the handle across your chest to the opposite shoulder. Hold for 3 seconds. Change sides and repeat.

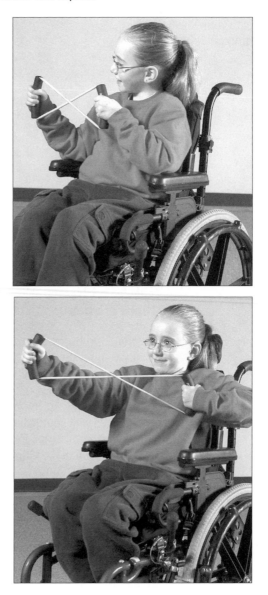

Front Butterfly

chest, back, shoulders

Instructions to children: Grasp the toner with both hands in front of your body, with your palms facing inward and your elbows slightly bent. Pull the toner out to each side. Hold for 3 seconds and return slowly to the starting position.

Back Butterfly

back, arms

Instructions to children: Grasp the handles with both hands overhead with your palms facing outward. Extend your arms downward, making the toner go behind your shoulders. Hold for 3 seconds and return slowly to the starting position.

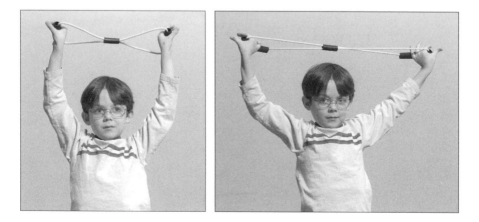

Side Pull

sides of abdomen, obliques

Instructions to children: Stand with your legs shoulder-width apart. Place one handle of the toner securely under your right foot and hold the other handle in your right hand with the palm facing your body. Now slide your left arm down your left leg, bending your body sideways toward the right. Stretch your right arm and fingers to reach toward the floor. Hold for 3 seconds and return to the starting position. Repeat on the opposite side.

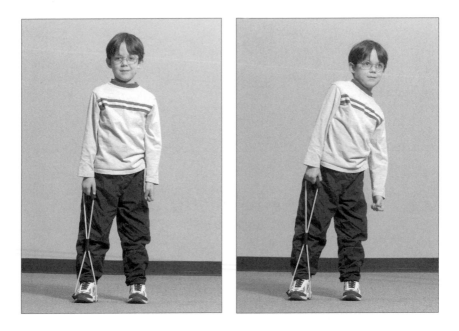

Band Exercises

The following exercises use the SPRI band, which is great for doing leg exercises. You can also use SPRI's Xering for leg exercises.

. . . . March Step . . . .

front of legs, hips

Instructions to children: Stand with your knees slightly bent, one leg in front of the other. Position the band around both ankles. Bend the knee of your front leg, lifting it several inches (centimeters) off the floor. Keep your hands on your hips and your trunk muscles tight. Slowly return to the starting position. Repeat on the opposite side.

. . . . Scissor Kick . . . .

back of legs

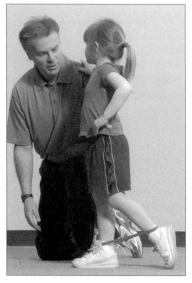

Instructions to children: Stand with one leg slightly in front of the other and position the band around both ankles. Balance on one foot or hold onto a chair or adult for support. Slowly lift and press the exercising leg backward, keeping the knee slightly bent. Point the toes downward, keeping your waist and lower back still. Slowly return to the starting position. Repeat on the opposite side.

.... Crossover Lift ....
inside of legs

Instructions to children: While standing, position the band around both legs. Place your hands on your hips or support yourself by grabbing a chair. Slowly lift and sweep the exercising leg across the front of your body, keeping the knee slightly bent. Rest your toes on the floor after each repetition.

Medicine Balls

Medicine balls are back in vogue. More than a hundred years ago, physicians used these weighted balls to help patients gain strength in their arms and shoulders after an injury—hence the term *medicine ball*. Today, these soft, pliable, and easy-to-use balls come in a variety of colors, weights, and sizes. This type of equipment is much safer to use than traditional dumbbells—and a lot more fun!

For ages four to six, use a 1.5-pound (0.7-kilogram), 6-inch- (15-centimeter-) diameter ball or a 2-pound (0.9-kilogram), 7-inch- (18-centimeter-) diameter ball. Children can exercise in pairs, on their own, or with a teacher or parent. *Note:* Medicine ball activities require close adult supervision and are not recommended for children under four years of age.

Toss and Catch

arms, shoulders

Instructions to children: Stand facing your partner so that you are about 2 feet (60 centimeters) apart. Both of you should have your feet about shoulder-width apart, with your knees slightly bent. Now toss the ball to your partner underhand (palms facing upward), then continue passing it back and forth a few times. When catching the ball, your knees should be slightly bent and your hands should be about 6 to 8 inches (15 to 20 centimeters) apart, palms facing upward.

Overhead Pass

arms, shoulders

Instructions to children: You and your partner stand back-to-back, about 6 inches (15 centimeters) apart, with your knees slightly bent. Start with the ball at your waist. At the signal "Begin," bring the ball up and over your head and pass it to your partner, then continue passing it back and forth a few times. When catching the ball, your hands should be about 6 to 8 inches (15 to 20 centimeters) apart with the palms facing upward.

trunk

Instructions to children: You and your partner stand back-to-back with your knees bent. Hold the ball at waist level. At the signal, both of you perform a slow half twist. You twist the ball to your left, and your partner twists to the right to accept the ball at waist level. Alternate sides and repeat the exercise.

. . . . **Rock and Roll** . . . .

arms, shoulders

Instructions to children: You and your partner face each other, about 3 feet (1 meter) apart, with your legs spread wide. Start by placing the medicine ball directly in front of you. Place your hands on the sides of the ball and slightly toward the back. Now rock slightly backward while holding the ball, then roll forward toward your partner. Your partner accepts the ball with extended arms and palms facing forward.

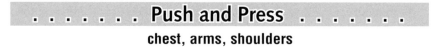

Push and Press

chest, arms, shoulders

Instructions to children: You stand holding a medicine ball with your knees slightly bent and your feet shoulder-width apart. Hold the ball at chest level, with your hands on the sides of it. Now push the ball straight out in front of you and bring it back to your chest. Repeat several times.

Stability Balls

Stability balls have been used by physical therapists for years, but now everyone—children, adults, and seniors—is realizing their benefits. These large, colorful, soft, pliable balls give kids a fun and exciting alternative for exercising. The information in this section should clear up any confusion about how to use stability balls and get you started performing the basics with your children.

Stability balls can be used to enhance flexibility, muscle fitness, balance, and posture. Children three to four years of age should use a ball inflated to a diameter of 14 inches (35 centimeters), and children five to six years of age should use a ball with a diameter of 18 inches (45 centimeters).

To meet the individual needs of children of different sizes and abilities, vary the ball size by slightly under- or overinflating it. Some stability balls come equipped with a pump specifically designed for them. To match ball sizes to individual children, the hips and knees should form a 90° angle when the child is seated on the ball.

All stability ball exercises should be done on a flat mat or padded carpet. To help keep children safe, the teacher or parent should stabilize the ball from behind with both hands until the child gains confidence in doing the exercises.

For more information, refer to *Kids on the Ball* by Anne Spalding, Linda Kelly, Janet Santopietro, and Joanne Posner-Mayer (1999).

. . . . Sitting and Smiling . . . .
back, sitting balance

Instructions to children: Sit in the center of the ball with your feet flat on the floor about shoulder-width apart. Gently hold onto the ball with both hands, one on each side. Keep your back straight and your head up. Now smile as wide as you can, make a funny face, look surprised, then close your eyes.

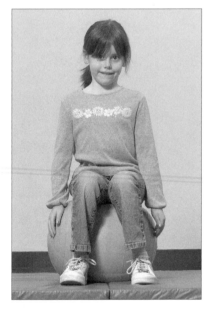

Sit-Fit

balance, arms, legs, trunk, back

Instructions to children: Sit correctly on the ball with your back straight and your feet flat on the floor with your knees at a 90° angle. Stay in that position and try the following arm and leg movements:

1. Airplane arms: Raise both arms and extend them out to the sides of your body like the wings of a plane.
2. Touchdown: Raise both arms overhead.
3. Right and left raise: Raise your right arm while gently holding the ball at the side with your left hand. Reverse arms and repeat the exercise.
4. Swimmer's stroke: Extend your right arm forward and hold your left arm back behind your head, with the elbow bent. Now alternate moving your arms in a swimmer's stroke. Bounce rhythmically to help keep you stable.
5. Egg beater: Make a fist with both hands and position them in front of you at chest level. Now rotate one fist over the other in a rhythmic fashion.
6. Heel taps: Extend your right leg forward with your heel on the floor and your toes pointing upward. Repeat with your left leg.
7. Toe taps: Extend your right leg sideways to the right and tap your right toe. Repeat with your left leg.
8. Leg extensions: Lift your right foot off the floor and extend your right leg forward, keeping your right knee slightly bent. Return slowly to the starting position. Repeat with your left leg. (See photo.)
9. Baby bounces: Begin doing small bounces by pushing your feet into the floor and slightly raising your hips. Keep control and bounce in a smooth, rhythmic manner.

back

Instructions to children: Begin by kneeling behind the ball. Now place your stomach across the center of the ball while holding onto it with both hands. Slowly straighten your arms out to your sides. Keep both feet on the floor. Hold for 3 to 5 seconds.

Advanced version: Try raising your chest a few inches (centimeters) off the ball.

Note: When spotting children, make sure they do not arch their back and that their hip remains on the ball.

. . . . **Back Extensions** . . . .

back

Instructions to children: Start by kneeling behind the ball and placing your stomach over the center of the ball. Keep your hands behind your head to support your neck, with your elbows pointing outward. Lift your upper torso off the ball while keeping your stomach on the ball. Hold for 2 to 3 seconds and return slowly to the starting position.

Note: Prevent children from interlocking their fingers when supporting the head and neck.

Walk Out

arms, shoulders, back, balance

Instructions to children: Start by kneeling behind the ball and placing your stomach over the center of the ball. Extend both arms forward, allowing the ball to roll under your body. Support your body by placing both hands flat on the floor. Now walk out until the ball is just under your ankles. Hold for 3 seconds and slowly walk your hands backward to the starting position.

Note: When children first try this exercise, they should be closely supervised by an adult, who should spot by holding the ball with both hands as the child walks out.

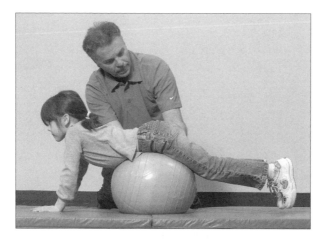

Back to Back

legs, trunk, cooperation

Pair up children of about equal size and have them stand back-to-back. Instruct them each to take a step forward while you place a stability ball firmly between their backs.

Instructions to children: Gently press the ball with your back to secure it between you and your partner. Try to walk in different directions while controlling the ball. Next, try to squeeze your stomach and bend your knees to a 90° angle, squatting down slowly. Hold for 3 seconds and return to the starting position.

. . . . Side by Side . . . .
legs, trunk, cooperation

This time, have two children stand side-by-side facing in opposite directions. Ask them to step away from each other while you place a stability ball between them.

Instructions to children: Each of you raise your left arm so your elbow is resting on the ball. Now squeeze and hold for several seconds.

Cardiorespiratory Endurance

Recall that cardiorespiratory endurance (CRE) is the capacity of the heart, blood vessels, and lungs to deliver nutrients and oxygen throughout the body to provide energy to run, jump, dance, swim, and so on. This component of health-related physical fitness is important during longer periods of active play.

Keep in mind, however, that higher-activity segments should be kept to short, intermittent bouts of about 2 to 3 minutes followed by 1 to 2 minutes of decreased physical activity or rest. This approach to CRE will also keep children actively involved, on task, and motivated to continue. Many of the activities in chapters 6 through 8 will enhance CRE.

Try these exciting CRE activities to get your children moving while helping them control their weight. You will need cones, jump ropes, a parachute, upbeat music, a CD or tape player, mats, large tires, hoops, and gym spots (often called **poly spots**).

Run for Fun

Designate a play area with cones or markers. Remind the children to stay within the boundaries. Play upbeat music. When the music starts, the children should start running in any direction at a moderate speed. When the music stops, the children should stop running.

Walk and Talk

Ask the children to find a friend in the group. Have the two- to three-year-olds join hands. Next, instruct the children to walk throughout the play area and talk to their friend. Suggest different topics or questions to help get the conversation started.

Walk in the Woods

Scatter plastic liter-sized bottles, cones, or Styrofoam cylinders throughout the play area to represent trees. Also create several rivers throughout the area by placing two jump ropes about 2 feet (60 centimeters) apart. Instruct the children to walk through the woods by avoiding the trees and rivers. When you call out "Rivers," the children have to walk to a river and jump over it, then continue to walk.

Jumping Joes

Spread several standard jump ropes on the floor, stretching them in a straight line. Assign one or two children per rope. Ask them to try the following:

- Walk around the rope
- Jog around the rope
- Skip around the rope
- Hop back and forth over the rope
- Hop back and forth as they travel down the length of the rope
- Hop back and forth over the rope on one leg
- Hop back and forth over the rope on one leg as they travel down the length of the rope
- Straddle the rope with both feet and hop down the length of the rope
- Make a half twist and jump and move in the opposite direction

Parachute Power

Have the children hold the parachute with one hand and begin to move counterclockwise. Play upbeat children's music, and ask the children to do the following movements in turn (change movements every 20 seconds):

- Walk
- Walk on their toes
- March step
- Walk briskly
- Walk slowly
- Take long steps
- Take short steps
- Hop
- Stop and jump up and down

Reinforce the cooperation among the group by stating, "Everyone is exercising and playing together. Great! Now let's go jog—together!"

Move to an open space and direct the children to hold onto the parachute with one hand. Ask them to walk in a certain direction together. (**Note:** You will have to join in and direct the children as well as set the pace.) When you feel they are moving as a group, ask them to start jogging.

Set up a circuit of various CRE activities in an open play space. Use arrows to remind the children the proper direction to follow. Review each station in the circuit and demonstrate the proper technique for performing the specific physical activities. Allow the children to move from one activity to another at their own pace.

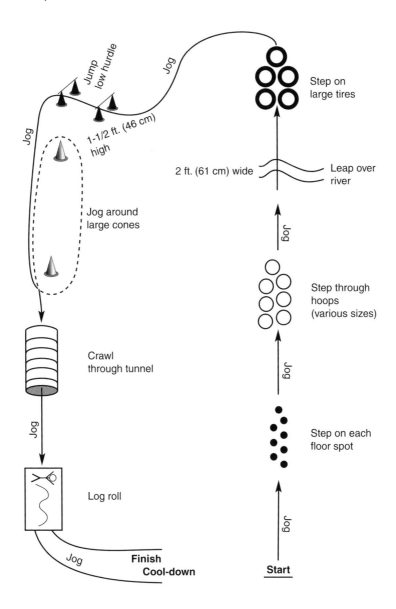

Step on large tires

Jump low hurdle

Jog

1-1/2 ft. (46 cm) high

Jog

2 ft. (61 cm) wide

Leap over river

Jog around large cones

Jog

Step through hoops (various sizes)

Crawl through tunnel

Jog

Step on each floor spot

Jog

Log roll

Jog   **Finish
Cool-down**

Jog

Start

Kids' Fitness Equipment

In 2002, Sport-Fun, Inc., launched the first series of physical activity equipment designed specifically for children ages two to six. The most popular items are the Start Walking Treadmill, the Start Pedaling Fitness Cycle, the Start Climbing Stepper, and the Start Pulling Rower. Each piece of equipment is colorful, foam coated, and kid-powered for safety. Parents have reported very positive results using the equipment at home.

"My child loves to hop on the cycle and watch cartoons—or exercise with me when I ride my stationary bike," says Bridget Roche of Huntington, New York.

Preschools have used the equipment to set up a fitness center in the corner of the room. Children use the equipment in short time segments throughout the day.

Photo courtesy of Sport-Fun.   Photo courtesy of Sport-Fun.

SUMMARY

Young children can and should participate in traditional types of exercise, but make sure the activity is age-appropriate and fun! Be mindful of the exercise guidelines and stages of a physical activity session described in this chapter as you select fitness activities for children. Use the numerous flexibility, muscles fitness, and cardiorespiratory endurance exercises to offer your children a wide and well-balanced variety of health-related physical fitness activities.

Chapter 6

© Cele Seldon

GO-GO GAMES

Games are an excellent way to increase **physical activity** levels in children ages two through six. Most children view playing active games as fun and exciting. Games are also a wonderful opportunity to develop social skills. Children learn how to lead, follow, take turns, cooperate, and support each other toward a common goal. Games are also helpful in developing mental skills such as listening, following directions, sequencing, making decisions, problem solving, and creating or modifying alternative solutions.

But games can place children under stress. Try to keep them fun and motivating without compromising sound educational principles. Thus, avoid games that eliminate players, cause embarrassment by isolating one child, include very little physical activity, or do little to reach your intended objectives.

10 CHARACTERISTICS
OF DEVELOPMENTAL GAMES

To maximize learning experiences, tailor games to the developmental level of the students. Simple modifications such as changing the boundaries of a game, varying the rules, or substituting a piece of equipment can ensure that all children are successful and are gaining the benefits of the game. Be mindful of the following 10 characteristics of a developmentally appropriate game. Refer to them from time to time to ensure that the games you select throughout the year are purposeful and enjoyable for all children.

1. Objective based: Each game should have an educational objective that supplies an instructional focus for the activity. Often children's games are played simply to fill time or to give children a break from more academic content. Note that each activity in this book has an educational objective or purpose such as increasing physical activity levels, teaching a skill, enhancing social interaction, and the like.

2. Fun: Children's games should always be fun. Moving about and playing lifts children's spirits and provides needed balance to their busy day. When games are fun, children come to view physical activity as positive and enjoyable, which fosters a lifelong core value about staying physically active. Laughing, giggling, cheering, and yelling should be encouraged!

3. Safe: Always make the safety of your children a top priority. Children should have safe, open spaces for highly active games. Establish proper buffer zones (about 8 feet [2.5 meters]) between play areas and obstacles (door, walls, etc.) and mark them clearly with bright orange cones. Check the playing surface daily to make sure it is level, dry, and free of debris. Check daily to ensure that children are wearing proper footwear (sneakers, sport socks) and are not wearing jewelry. Teach children to move in their own personal space and to respect the space of others. Teach them how to stop, start, and change direction while watching other children and their environment.

4. No human targets: Physical education equipment should never be used to throw or kick at other children. Teach children that balls, beanbags, Frisbees, and the like are used to develop skills, not to target other game participants.

5. Inclusive: Games should include every child in class at all times. Modify the rules, equipment, or game procedures to ensure that every child is an active participant capable of success. No matter whether children have disabilities, are obese, or are lacking in skills, they should be included and made to feel a part of any game activity. Also, during a game, never eliminate a player for being unsuccessful. Find a way to keep them involved. Children learn skills by doing, not by watching or listening.

6. Engaging: Children should spend most of the time on task in a game situation. If children are standing in lines or are otherwise uninvolved, they will not gain the benefits of the game. For example,

in the game Duck, Duck, Goose, most of the children are sitting uninvolved much of the time—time that could be better spent moving, catching, throwing, kicking, and the like. A simple tag game is much more beneficial because it keeps all children moving and involved.

7. Active: Games are ideal tools for raising the activity levels of children. Ask yourself this simple question: "Do all of my students have the opportunity to move continuously throughout the game?" Active games are excellent ways for children to accumulate 15 to 20 minutes of moderate to vigorous physical activity every day. Be sure to break active games into short intervals of about 3 to 4 minutes with intermittent rest periods throughout the activity.

8. Use appropriate equipment and facilities: Game equipment should always match the developmental needs of the learner. Try to provide your class with various sizes and shapes of equipment to match the skill levels. For example, foam bats should be oversized, paddles should be lightweight with properly sized grips, and balls should be made of foam or yarn and be easy to grasp and handle. Also, constantly reassess the play area and game boundaries for compatibility with the developmental level as well as safety precautions. Try to use standard equipment from a reliable manufacturer to avoid injury and potential lawsuits.

9. Teach cooperation: Active games are excellent vehicles for teaching children about cooperation. Take the time during a game to point out how well children are sharing, respecting each other, and playing safely. Emphasize these characteristics rather than the competitiveness of the game.

10. Positive competition: Most games require a certain amount of competition. To create a positive experience, focus on the game objectives—skills improvement, physical activity benefits, and enjoyment of the game—rather than on which individual or team did the best.

Also, reinforce the importance of active games in providing health benefits such as strong legs and arms and a healthy heart. For example, ask children to feel their heartbeat before they play a game and then again directly afterward. Explain to them that the heart is a very important muscle of the body and that active games will keep their heart strong and healthy. Teach children to view games as healthy, fun activities experienced with their peers rather than as competitive events between friends and classmates.

Jungle Animals . . . . Ages 2 to 3

>>> Objectives

Creative, expressive movement, **fundamental movement skills**

>>> Participants

6 to 12 children

>>> Equipment and Materials

Construction paper, scissors, animal pictures

>>> Description

Divide the class in half and develop two identical sets of pictures of animals, one for each group; each set should contain the same number of pictures as there are children in the group. Place the pictures in two large bags. Arrange the children in two parallel lines about 40 to 50 feet (12 to 15 meters) apart. Walk along the lines and have the students in each line select a picture from their group bag (No peeking!).

At the signal to start, have the children walk, crawl, or move toward each other imitating the animal they selected and making the corresponding animal noises as well (oinking like a pig, barking like a dog, hissing like a snake, whinnying like a horse, etc.).

The objective of the game is for children to find their counterpart from the other group. Once they do so, the two of them stand together and continue to imitate the sound and movement of the animal.

>>> Modifications

Repeat the procedure several times to ensure that children get a chance to imitate a different animal each round.

Crows and Cranes . . . . Ages 2 to 6

>>> *Objectives*

Increase physical activity levels, improve fleeing and chasing skills

>>> *Participants*

8 to 12 children

>>> *Equipment and Materials*

Four cones

>>> *Description*

Divide the class into two groups—crows and cranes—and have the groups line up facing each other about 5 to 6 feet (1.5 to 2 meters) apart. Behind each group of children, use the cones to mark a line approximately 30 yards (27.5 meters) from the starting point of the game. This will be the safety line for each group.

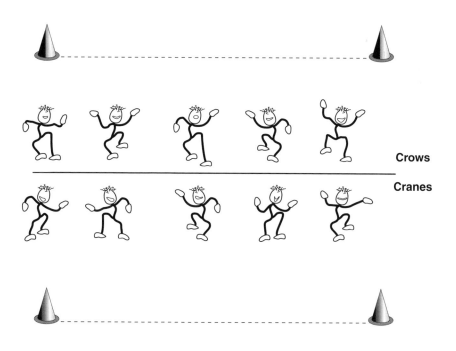

Crows

Cranes

Stand at one end of the lines and call out either "Crows!" or "Cranes!" If you call "Crows," the crows run and are chased by the cranes. If a crow is tagged by a crane before he reaches his own safety line, located directly behind him, he becomes a crane. Conversely, if you call "Cranes," the cranes are chased by the crows.

⫸ Modifications

To heighten the excitement, you can draw out the "Crows" and "Cranes" calls by stretching the "cr-r-r-r-r-r" sound before completing the word. Each round can be modified by having the children perform a different motor skill (e.g., skipping, hopping, crawling).

Shape Around . . . . Ages 2 to 6

>>> Objectives

Increase physical activity levels, creative movement

>>> Participants

4 to 12 children

>>> Equipment and Materials

None

>>> Description

Arrange the children in a circle. Start by asking one of the children to create any movement she likes. Next, have the entire group imitate the movement. Then ask the next child to do the same, with all children imitating the movement. Be sure that all the children in the circle get a chance to create a movement. If a child is unsure or shy, you can suggest a new movement.

>>> Modifications

Ask the children to imitate animal movements. Use music to motivate participation in this activity.

Parachute Golf . . . . Ages 2 to 6

≫ Objectives
Muscular fitness, cooperation

≫ Participants
4 to 12 children

≫ Equipment and Materials
Small- or medium-sized **parachute** (depending on group size) with a center hole

≫ Description
Space children evenly around the parachute and ask them to grasp the handles using an overhand grip. Place a medium-sized ball (6- to 8-inch [15- to 20-centimeter] diameter) inside the parachute. The objective is for the group to maneuver the ball around the parachute to get it to fall through the center hole. Demonstrate to the group that as one side raises the chute, the other side lowers it to help direct the ball toward the hole. Reinforce the need to cooperate and work as a team to get the ball through the hole.

≫ Modifications
Ask the children to move counterclockwise as a group, first walking, then jogging, and then skipping, while trying to pass the ball through the hole in the center of the parachute.

Safari . . . . Ages 2 to 6

>>> Objectives

Increase physical activity levels, vary exercises and locomotor movements

>>> Participants

4 to 12 children

>>> Equipment and Materials

Gym **poly spots** (more than the number of children in the group) or paper plates, scissors, pictures of animals, tape, jungle music, CD or tape player

>>> Description

Explain to the children that they will be moving throughout the "jungle" looking for animals. Tape pictures of jungle animals to the underside of each poly spot or paper plate and spread them throughout the play area.

When the jungle music begins, direct the children to move around the play area using various locomotor movements (walking, jogging, skipping). When the music stops, the children find a poly spot, turn it over, and imitate the animal movements (e.g., monkey, tiger, elephant, snake, alligator, bird).

>>> Modifications

Decorate the play area with jungle pictures. You might want to wear a safari hat.

⋙ Objectives

Increase physical activity levels, following directions and moving in different pathways

⋙ Participants

2 to 10 children

⋙ Equipment and Materials

30 to 40 cones, markers, or gym tape; cutout green "go" signs, red "stop" signs, and yellow "slow" signs; tape; scissors; one plastic or rubber ring for each child

⋙ Description

Design a roadway course in an open area. Use cones to designate the driving lanes. Have the children negotiate the course, pretending that the plastic or rubber ring is the car steering wheel. Place a green sign at the start of the course and red and yellow signs at several intersections. When approaching a "Stop" sign, the children must come to a complete stop, look both ways, and follow the pathway. Yellow signs mean "slow down" (walk slowly). Students are only allowed to jog, not sprint, and they may not pass other students or go in reverse.

Have each child go through the course three or four times. At the end of the activity, provide cups of water for each child to reinforce the point that, just like a car, our bodies get overheated and need water.

⋙ Modifications

Give each child a different-colored label denoting various car makes.

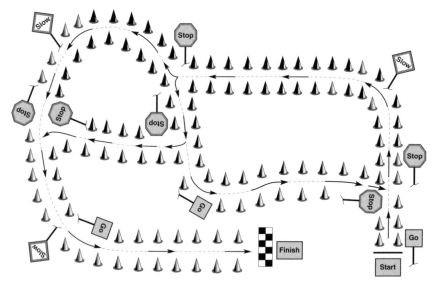

Hoop Around . . . . Ages 2 to 6

>>> *Objectives*

Increase physical activity levels, fundamental **locomotor skills**, color identification

>>> *Participants*

6 to 12 children

>>> *Equipment and Materials*

12 large colored hoops—at least two of each color (red, yellow, blue); upbeat children's music; CD or tape player

>>> *Description*

Scatter the hoops throughout the play area. Instruct each child to stand outside one of the hoops. Start the music and call out a command for the children to begin performing a locomotor movement (e.g., "March like a soldier!").

After 30 seconds of locomotor movement, stop the music and call out a color—red, yellow, or blue—signaling the children to run to a hoop of that color and stand inside it. Be sure to have at least two hoops of each primary color to avoid crowding.

Then start the music again and call out another command (e.g., "Hop like a rabbit!"), allowing 30 seconds of movement before calling out another primary color.

>>> *Modifications*

Ask children to place only one body part in the hoop when the color is called (e.g., toes, head, elbow, fingers, or wrist).

Whistle Mixer . . . . Ages 2 to 6

>>> Objectives

Increase physical activity levels, locomotor skills, social interaction

>>> Participants

6 to 15 children

>>> Equipment and Materials

Whistle

>>> Description

Instruct children to scatter themselves throughout an open play area. Begin by asking them to walk around the area and smile. Then ask them to walk taking giant steps and then baby steps.

Next, blow two short blasts on the whistle as a signal for the children to run and get into pairs. Then ask them to jog around the play area. When they hear three whistle blasts, the children form a circle of three and hold hands. Do not go above a count of four, as it gets too confusing for children.

Avoid calling attention to any children without a group; simply keep the game going with the next movement (skipping, hopping, etc.).

>>> Modifications

Stretch the movement time segments for increased physical activity; about 15 seconds is usually sufficient for two- to three-year-olds and 20 seconds for four- to six-year-olds. Try using four or five whistle blasts with the five- and six-year-old children.

Scarf Tag . . . . Ages 2 to 6

>>> Objectives

Crawling skills, fleeing and chasing

>>> Participants

4 to 12 children

>>> Equipment and Materials

Scarf, handkerchief, or small rag for each child; carpeted area; several small plastic cones; upbeat music; CD or tape player; box with several extra scarves

>>> Description

Instruct all children to tuck the scarf into the sneaker on their left foot, allowing about 6 to 8 inches (15 to 20 centimeters) to stick out on the outside of their foot. Ask the children to get into a crawling position supported on their hands and knees. Set boundaries within the play area using small plastic cones.

When the music begins (or on the "Go" signal), the children must move around and try to avoid getting their scarf pulled while trying to pull other children's scarves from their sneakers. If a child loses her scarf, she must go over to the scarf box and get another one, then continue to play.

>>> Modifications

Try various movements such as walking like a bear. When playing outdoors or in an open play area, the children may tuck the scarf into the waistband of their pants and run, skip, or hop, trying to pull out the scarf of another child.

Moving Pictures . . . . Ages 2 to 6

>>> Objectives

Locomotor skills, moving in general space, relationships

>>> Participants

4 to 12 children

>>> Equipment and Materials

Camera, 4- by 6-inch (10- by 15-centimeter) index cards in two colors

>>> Description

Begin by taking photographs of five objects on the playground (monkey bars, oak tree, fence) to serve as destinations. Also, take five photographs of children performing various types (methods) of movement such as hopping, crawling, or walking. Label the photos and mount them on different-colored cards—one color for object cards (destination) and the other color for method cards (movement type).

Divide the class into two groups according to card type. Invite one of the children to choose an object card and call out the destination. Invite another child to select a method card and call out the movement type. Then call out "Moving pictures!" to signal all children to move to the destination using the movement method selected.

Be sure that all children get a chance to select a card. In the next round, have the children change groups (the object card group becomes the method card group).

>>> Modifications

Change environments; this activity can be done indoors, but make sure the area is clear of obstacles and hazards.

Squirrels in Trees . . . . Ages 4 to 6

>>> *Objectives*

Increase physical activity levels, fundamental locomotor skills

>>> *Participants*

6 to 12 children

>>> *Equipment and Materials*

Crepe paper, scissors

>>> *Description*

Cut strips of white crepe paper about 2 feet (60 centimeters) in length and tuck them into the back of each player's waistband to represent a tail.

Divide the players into groups of three and assign them the numbers 1, 2, and 3. Numbers 1 and 2 join hands to form a tree; number 3 is the squirrel and stands inside the tree formed by numbers 1 and 2. Position the trees around an open area at least 15 yards (13.5 meters) apart.

Start the game by calling out "Squirrels change trees!" The trees raise their arms to allow the squirrel to move to another tree and another squirrel to enter. Only one squirrel is allowed per tree.

If there is an extra squirrel or two in the group (i.e., the group cannot be divided equally), allow the extra squirrel to call out the next motor skill the squirrels must use to get to a tree (for example, "Skip!" "Hop!" "March!"), or simply keep the game moving to avoid calling attention to any squirrels who are unable to find a tree.

>>> *Modifications*

Vary the game by calling out "Trees change, squirrels stay in place!" This time, the trees separate, find another squirrel, and form a tree around it.

Three Touches . . . . Ages 4 to 6

>>> *Objectives*

Locomotor skills, thinking skills, sequencing

>>> *Participants*

2 to 12 children

>>> *Equipment and Materials*

Standard objects at home, school, or on the playground; upbeat music; CD or tape player

>>> *Description*

Establish the play area and set boundaries. Explain to the children that they will be touching any three things in the room or on the playground and must try to remember the things they touch. Provide examples of possible touches (chair, desk, door, water fountain, fence, monkey bars, crawling tunnel). When the music begins, have the children walk around the room finding objects to touch. When they have touched three objects, they return to a designated spot.

Ask each child the following questions: "Can you remember what you touched?" "Can you remember the order in which you touched the objects?"

>>> *Modifications*

Change the locomotor skills each time the children move. Try increasing the touches to four or five with the six-year-olds. Also, ask the children to select different objects each time you begin a new round.

Heart to Heart . . . . Ages 4 to 6

>>> Objectives

Increase physical activity levels, body part identification, heart location and size

>>> Participants

8 to 12 children

>>> Equipment and Materials

Upbeat children's music; CD or tape player

>>> Description

Teach children where their heart is located and have them feel their heartbeat. Ask them to make a fist and hold it over their heart. Explain to the children that this is the size of the heart in their chest and that it is a very important muscle that helps them run, jump, skip, and hop.

Position the children about 3 feet (1 meter) apart throughout the play area. Start the music and call out a locomotor movement for the children to perform (e.g., "Skip!"); when the music stops, call out a body part that they must match with another student in the class ("Back to back"). Then call out another locomotor movement ("Hop!") and start the music again. Continue calling out locomotor movements, stopping the music, and calling out body parts to match ("Toes to toes!" "Elbow to elbow!" "Knee to knee!"). At the end of the activity, call out "Heart to heart." When this signal is called, have the children make a fist with their right hand and hold it over the left side of their chest. Instruct the children to stand left shoulder to left shoulder as a symbolic "heart to heart."

>>> Modifications

Play this game during the month of February as a tie-in to Heart Health Month and Valentine's Day. When the children complete the activity, tape cutout hearts to the left side of each child's chest to remind them of the activity and to show to their parents after school.

Rolling for Fitness . . . . Ages 4 to 6

>>> Objectives

Increase physical activity levels, locomotor skills, warm-up activity, counting skills

>>> Participants

15 children

>>> Equipment and Materials

Foam die, upbeat children's music, CD or tape player

>>> Description

Have children form a large circle and place the die in the middle. Ask the children to begin walking counterclockwise. When the music stops, call out the name of a child in the class. The child must run to the middle to roll the die and count the number of spots on the side facing up (e.g., three). Next, call out an exercise that all the children must perform three times (three long jumps, three short hops, or three toe raises).

Each time the children begin to move around the circle again, change the locomotor skill.

>>> Modifications

Some children may be able to use two dice and count to 12, but you may have to help. This motivating activity can be used as a 5-minute warm-up before another planned activity.

Farmers and Lumberjacks . . . . Ages 4 to 6

>>> Objectives

Increase physical activity levels, body part identification

>>> Participants

6 to 12 children

>>> Equipment and Materials

10 to 16 standard cones (there should be several more cones than the number of players in the game), upbeat music, CD or tape player

>>> Description

Scatter the cones throughout the play area. Knock over half of the cones so they are lying on their sides. Divide the group into two teams, designating one team as "farmers" and the other as "lumberjacks."

Explain to the children that when the music begins, the lumberjacks will try to knock over the cones (to simulate lumberjacks cutting down trees in the forest) and the farmers will try to pick up the cones (to simulate farmers growing fruits and vegetables).

Continue the activity for 30 seconds and have the children change roles (farmers become lumberjacks and vice versa).

>>> Modifications

Ask the lumberjacks to knock down the cones using various body parts (elbow, knee, or foot).

⟫⟫ *Objectives*

Increase physical activity levels, reinforce fish as a healthy food

⟫⟫ *Participants*

6 to 12 children

⟫⟫ *Equipment and Materials*

Two plastic laundry baskets, string, cardboard or heavy construction paper cut into the shape of fish, hole punch, scissors, 12 felt markers in various colors

⟫⟫ *Description*

Begin by cutting about 30 fish designs out of cardboard or construction paper, and ask the children to decorate them. Punch a hole near the mouth of each fish and attach a long string to it. Tuck the end of the string into the back of each child's waistband. The fish should hang about 12 to 16 inches (30 to 40 centimeters) from the child's waist. Label the two baskets as "Caught Fish" and "Live Bait" and place several cutout fish in them. Spread the baskets about 15 to 20 yards (13.5 to 18 meters) apart. On the "Go" signal, each child

attempts to go fishing by pulling the fish from another child's waistband. When they "catch" a fish, they take it to the "Caught Fish" basket and continue to play. When a child loses his fish, he jogs to the "Live Bait" basket and gets another fish tucked into his waistband, then continues to play. At the end of the game, explain to the children that eating fish is a healthy eating habit. We should all eat fish twice per week as recommended by the American Heart Association (2004).

≫ Modifications

Label each fish by type (e.g., salmon, shark, flounder, red snapper, catfish) and shape the cutouts to resemble each type. Try laminating the fish to preserve them for use throughout the year.

Busy Bees . . . . Ages 4 to 6

>>> *Objectives*

Increase physical activity, moving in open space in different directions

>>> *Participants*

8 to 12 children

>>> *Equipment and Materials*

Four hoops, 25 pieces of various equipment (e.g., beanbags, small cones, rubber rings, yarn balls)

>>> *Description*

Divide the children into three or four groups of busy bees and assign them hula hoops as their beehives. Spread the pieces of equipment throughout the open play area. Explain to the children that they are to pretend they are worker bees and their beehive (hoop) is out of honey. After a few minutes, call "Go bees!" to signal the children to run to the middle of the open space and collect "honey" (pieces of equipment), one piece at a time, then bring the honey (balls, rings, beanbags) back to their beehive as fast as possible.

When you call "Rain," all bees must return to their beehives. The children then count the pieces of equipment (honey) in their beehive.

>>> *Modifications*

Change locomotor movements for each round (walking, jogging, skipping, hopping).

Changing Leaders . . . . Ages 4 to 6

>>> Objectives

Increase physical activity levels, imitate various locomotor movements

>>> Participants

4 to 12 children

>>> Equipment and Materials

Upbeat children's music, CD or tape player

>>> Description

Arrange the children in groups of three or four and designate a line leader for each group. When the music starts, the children in each line must imitate the line leaders' movements as the lines travel throughout the play space.

Leaders can perform any safe movement (march steps, crawling, hopping). When the music stops momentarily, call "Change!" The line keeps moving, but the last child in each line jogs to the front and becomes the new line leader, performing a new movement for the line to imitate.

>>> Modifications

Suggest various movements or animal imitations to children who are having difficulty thinking of a new movement.

››› Objectives

Guessing game, locomotor skills, creative movements

››› Participants

4 to 12 children

››› Equipment and Materials

Upbeat children's music, CD or tape player

››› Description

Arrange a group of children in a circle and ask one child (fitness guesser) to leave the area or cover her eyes. Next, select an exercise leader and explain that he is to change the activity at any time throughout the session but that he must do so with his actions alone, rather than by speaking or calling out the new activity. Then ask the fitness guesser to come back into the play area while the children are moving. The fitness guesser must try to guess who is changing the exercises or movements and identify the fitness leader.

››› Modifications

You can help the leader think of various movements before the guesser arrives. Instead of using a circle format, have the children scatter throughout the play area to make things more difficult for the fitness guesser.

Hunters and Buffaloes . . . . . Ages 4 to 6

>>> Objectives

Increase physical activity levels, moving in open space

>>> Participants

6 to 12 children

>>> Equipment and Materials

None

>>> Description

Designate the play area as an open pasture or field where the buffalo roam. Select one or two hunters; the rest of the group are buffaloes.

Instruct the buffaloes to begin roaming around the play area. Next, call out various locomotor movements for the buffaloes to perform (walking, skipping, hopping, galloping, etc.). Then call out "Buffalo hunt!" to signal the hunters to jog around trying to tag the buffaloes.

Buffaloes that get tagged must lie on their backs with their arms and legs in the air. A healthy buffalo can revive a tagged buffalo by tapping both their hands and feet while reciting, "Go, buffalo! Go, buffalo! Go, buffalo!" While this is being done, the two buffaloes involved are safe and cannot be tagged. Rotate the hunters every few minutes.

>>> Modifications

The hunters can wear Native American headdresses.

Blob Tag . . . . Ages 4 to 6

≫ Objectives

Increase physical activity levels, cooperative skills

≫ Participants

6 to 12 children

≫ Equipment and Materials

None

≫ Description

Select one child to be "it" and have the rest of the children scatter throughout the play area. At the "Go" signal, the child who is "it" tries to tag other children. The tagged children join one hand and together try to tag the other children. The line gets longer and longer as more children are tagged. The children on both ends of the line become the taggers, closing in on other children.

Now the line (blob) must work together and cooperate as they move toward the free children. Continue play until only a few children are free, then begin a new round with a different "it."

≫ Modifications

Ask the free children to perform various locomotor skills as they flee from the blob. Emphasize how all the children in the blob have to cooperate to chase the free children.

SUMMARY

To maximize the benefits of various games, keep in mind the elements of a developmentally appropriate game activity. The games described in this chapter will help you increase the physical activity levels of your children each day. They require little equipment and can be easily implemented by any adult.

Games will also help promote cooperation among your children and underscore the importance of social interaction through **play.**

Chapter 7

SKILLS AND THRILLS

Children enjoy learning new motor skills; they love to catch, throw, kick, and strike. But motor skills need to be taught to children carefully, and they need the time to reinforce and practice skills throughout childhood. This chapter describes a framework of developmental **movement concepts** and **movement themes**. It also provides essential guidelines in the form of seven simple principles of skill development, as well as a variety of practical activities to keep children motivated.

The motivation to learn new skills should be nurtured and supported as children develop. Thus, how you interact with children between the ages of two and six is as important as the skills you teach. The focus should always remain on a child's individual needs rather than on the specific skills. At this level, performance should not be a priority, and competition may actually hinder skill development. Developing new physical skills will help children stay active as they move through early childhood. It may also establish movement patterns that will last for many years, helping children create a healthy lifestyle and control their weight throughout their lives.

The skills presented to children between ages two and six will serve as building blocks for more advanced skills later in elementary school.

The emphasis should be on movement concepts, or how a movement is performed, such as space awareness (self-space, general space, directions, levels, and pathways), effort (time, force, flow), and relationships (body parts, with objects, with people).

The concepts of movement should be integrated throughout the core movement themes (**locomotor**, **nonlocomotor**, and **manipulative skills**), movements that are performed or executed.

Locomotor Skills

- Walking
- Running
- Hopping
- Leaping
- Sliding
- Galloping
- Skipping

Nonlocomotor Skills

- Bending
- Twisting
- Turning
- Rocking and swaying
- Balancing
- Stretching
- Pushing
- Pulling

Manipulative Skills

- Rolling
- Throwing
- Catching
- Striking
- Volleying
- Kicking
- Punting
- Trapping
- Dribbling

SEVEN SIMPLE PRINCIPLES OF SKILL DEVELOPMENT

Follow these seven simple principles when organizing skills-related activities for your children:

1. Have patience. You must remain patient as children explore various skill activities. They will be unsuccessful and at times will look awkward, but they are still learning. Repeat a skills activity intermittently throughout the year rather than give up because children are not able to show competence.

2. Maximize time on task. Children need time to create, explore, and practice. Skills-related activity should be scheduled every day for children between the ages of two and six. Try to give children repeated rounds or turns to help establish a skill pattern.

3. Teach skills, not performance. Focus on the benefits of the movement concepts and skill themes rather than on how well a child is performing the skill. Competitive activities, measuring skill accuracy, and providing feedback on performance may have an adverse effect on skill development. The purpose of game-related activity should be to practice skills rather than accentuate competitiveness.

4. Optimize class size and equipment. Limiting group size is important to ensure that each child has the opportunity to move freely in a safe, supportive environment. A group size of 12 is typical, depending on space and equipment available. According to standards established by the National Association for Sport and Physical Education (NASPE 2000) and the National Association for the Education of Young Children (NAEYC 1997), the optimum group size for three-year-olds is no more than 16 children with two adults and for four-year-olds is no more than 20 children with two adults.

   Equipment should be matched to each child's developmental level. Use of lightweight equipment such as balls, bats, and paddles tends to enhance children's manipulative skills as well as their self-confidence in **physical activity**. When possible, purchase equipment from a reputable company rather than relying on homemade equipment that may be unsafe (see appendix A).

5. Be success oriented. When children are happy and successfully learning new skills, they will be motivated to continue the activity. Studies indicate that children should be successful about 80% of the time to establish a positive pattern in the movement environment (Sanders 2002).

6. Promote active learning. Allow children to be active learners. Organize activities to provide them the opportunity to make choices. Also allow children to make decisions and create their own games or skill activities. They will feel more self-directed, and learning will take on a more personal meaning.

7. Provide variety. Try to offer a wide variety of movement skills to children (refer to the skill concepts or themes outlined earlier in this chapter). Provide them with a balance of structured and unstructured activity time throughout the day, and plan for indoor as well as outdoor activity. Constantly look for ways to liven up your program with innovative activities and equipment, rather than relying on the same old standards (e.g., "red light, green light") year in and year out.

Body Shaping . . . . Ages 2 to 3

⋙ *Objectives*

Body awareness

⋙ *Participants*

One child per outline

⋙ *Equipment and Materials*

Large sheets of butcher paper, crayons, markers

⋙ *Description*

Have a child lie on his back on a large sheet of butcher paper with arms and legs outstretched.

Trace an outline of the child's entire body. When you have finished tracing the outline, ask the child to create and color various body parts such as feet, toes, hands, fingers, nose, and eyes. As you help the child color in the outline, reinforce learning of the body parts by labeling each major body part. Write the child's first name at the top of the completed outline and display it around the room.

Next, invite all the children to shake, wiggle, or move the various body parts as you call them out.

⋙ *Modifications*

Trace outlines of the children in various body postures—one arm up and one down, legs bent to form a triangle, legs straight, and so on.

The Spider Crawl . . . . Ages 2 to 3

>>> Objectives
Expressive movement, levels

>>> Participants
Six to eight children

>>> Equipment and Materials
Long pieces of thick yarn, rope, or cord

>>> Description
Arrange four or five children in a circle and have them stand with their legs spread apart. Instruct the children to grasp the string with their fingers as you crisscross it back and forth across the circle to form a web. Once the web has been formed, assign two or three other children the role of spiders. On the signal "Spiders crawling," the spiders crawl under the spider web to the other side. After a few minutes, have the spiders change places with the children holding the web so that everyone gets a chance at playing both roles.

>>> Modifications
Take a walk outside or explore the room trying to find real spider webs.

Gumbo . . . . Ages 2 to 3

>>> Objectives

Personal space, cooperation

>>> Participants

Four to six children

>>> Equipment and Materials

Cutout pictures of various food items used to make gumbo (carrots, okra, greens, potatoes, chicken, and cayenne pepper), Cajun music, CD or tape player, mask materials (paper plates, feathers, glue sticks, crayons, glitter, and large craft sticks)

>>> Description

Explain that gumbo is a southern Louisiana soup that includes many ingredients. Arrange the children in a tightly formed circle. Next, identify each child with a different ingredient—carrot, okra, greens, potato, chicken, spices—by taping a large cutout of it to the child's shirt.

Instruct the children to wiggle, shake, and bob up and down when you call out the signal "Cook!" Periodically call out "Gumbo!" to signal the children to join arms and give each other a group hug. Then call out "Cook!" again to signal the children to step back and resume wiggling and shaking.

>>> Modifications

Prepare gumbo as a meal for the children (leave out the Cajun sausage!). Discuss the healthy ingredients used to make gumbo and reinforce the importance of eating healthy foods. To add excitement to the activity, schedule it around Mardi Gras. Complete the theme by having each child create a Mardi Gras mask using a paper plate and craft materials.

Strike-o-Rama . . . . Ages 2 to 6

>>> *Objectives*

Striking skills

>>> *Participants*

1 to 12 children

>>> *Equipment and Materials*

Cones, foam bats, paddles, hockey sticks, balloons, beach balls, foam noodles, foam balls, carpet squares

>>> *Description*

This activity introduces the manipulative skill of striking with a variety of long-handled objects such as paddles, bats, foam noodles, and hockey sticks. Set up a series of stations around the play area, allowing each child several minutes to practice each skill. Assign no more than two children per station. Be sure to have enough equipment to accommodate all the children.

Suggested Station Activities

1. Striking a 4- to 6-inch- (10- to 15-centimeter-) diameter foam ball off a tee (cone) using an oversized foam bat (Place the cone about 10 yards [9 meters] from the wall.)
2. Striking a balloon for distance using a foam hockey stick
3. Striking suspended beach balls or balloons with a foam wand (noodle)
4. Striking a 4- to 6-inch- (10- to 15-centimeter-) diameter foam ball through a goal with a foam hockey stick
5. Striking a balloon with a foam paddle (self-toss and strike with the other hand)
6. Striking a balloon with various body parts—hands, wrists, elbows, head—and trying to keep it from touching the ground

Safety: Spread the stations throughout the play area and use boundary markers such as orange cones to keep children from drifting into another activity area. Position carpet squares on the left and right sides of certain stations to designate where the children should stand while performing the activity. You may need a few aides to help out at the stations.

>>> *Modifications*

Try using various pieces of equipment such as plastic croquet mallets, plastic golf clubs, and brooms to enhance striking skills.

Rolling Bowling . . . . Ages 2 to 6

>>> Objectives
Rolling skills

>>> Participants
Two children per alley

>>> Equipment and Materials
Slant boards for each pair of children; two sturdy boxes; bowling pins, liter-sized soda bottles, or milk cartons; 8 1/2-inch- (22-centimeter-) diameter rubber ball for each pair of children

>>> Description
Arrange the slant boards by supporting them on two sturdy boxes or a chair. Assign two children per slant board or alley.

Set up at least four targets at the bottom of the board, such as milk cartons, soda bottles, or plastic bowling pins. Have each child take a turn rolling the ball from the top of the slant board to see how many targets she can knock over.

>>> Modifications
Try placing the targets farther away from the bottom of the board as the children become more competent in this activity.

>>> **Objectives**

Passing skills

>>> **Participants**

3 to 12 children

>>> **Equipment and Materials**

Various items to be passed: rubber heart, healthy snack, foam ball, stuffed animal, beanbag, small box with a lid; upbeat music; CD or tape player

>>> **Description**

Group children in circles, with no more than six per circle, and ask them to sit down. Start the music and instruct the children to begin passing around an item. When the music stops, the child holding the item must perform a specific task. For example:

- Heart Thump: The child holding the rubber heart places it over the left side of her chest.
- Healthy Snack: The child holding the healthy snack gets to keep it for snack time (play until all children have a snack).
- Ball of Fun: The child holding the foam ball tells the group what he likes to do with the ball.
- Furry Friend: The child holding the small stuffed animal gets to give it a big hug.
- Hot Tamale: The child holding the beanbag (tamale) gets to toss it up in the air and catch it to cool it off.
- Surprise, Surprise: The child holding the small box with the lid takes a guess at what's inside (give hints).

>>> **Modifications**

Five- and six-year-olds can move in a circle while passing various items.

Keep It Up . . . . Ages 2 to 6

>>> Objectives

Striking skills, body part identification

>>> Participants

Two to four children

>>> Equipment and Materials

Large balloons, a beach ball for each child, upbeat music, CD or tape player

>>> Description

Give each child a balloon or beach ball. The purpose of this activity is to see how many times the children can strike the balloon and keep it in the air before it touches the ground. After a few minutes, ask the children to keep the ball in the air using various body parts: wrists, elbows, knees, fist, and so on. Play upbeat music to keep the activity moving. When the music stops, the children secure their balloons and sit down.

>>> Modifications

Five- and six-year-olds will enjoy forming a circle of three or four children. Start with one balloon and see how many times the group can strike the balloon before it touches the ground. Ask them to shout out the number each time they are successful. Then play again to see if they can beat their previous score. Add another balloon once the children have developed the activity skills.

Sports Models . . . . Ages 2 to 6

>>> Objectives
Expressive movement

>>> Participants
2 to 12 children

>>> Equipment and Materials
Sports theme music (e.g., "Jock Jams," ESPN Music, 2004), CD or tape player

>>> Description
Position children in their own personal space throughout the play area. Use sports themes as background music. Ask the children to pretend to be sports models by imitating certain skills. Prompt them with verbal cues:

- "Who can make believe they are a basketball player dribbling a ball?"
- "Now shoot at the basket. Yeah, you scored!"
- "Now, let's see if you can be a pitcher in a baseball game. You struck out the batter! Great!"
- "Now be the batter. Wow! You hit a home run! Now run the bases."
- "Can you show me a football throw? Throw a long pass . . . now catch it . . . run, run, run for a touchdown!"
- "Let me see you kick the soccer ball around the area. Use one foot, then the other. Now kick it hard. Great job! You scored a goal!"

>>> Modifications
For more exciting activities, purchase Greg and Steve "Sports Dance," produced by Youngheart Records, P.O. Box 27784, Los Angeles, CA 90027.

Maze Mania . . . . Ages 2 to 6

>>> Objectives

Spatial awareness, directions, pathways, problem solving

>>> Participants

2 to 12 children

>>> Equipment and Materials

Several folding mats, cones, hoops, pillows, relaxing music, CD or tape player

>>> Description

Stand several folding mats on edge throughout the play space, folding the sections of the mats to create a maze. Make sure the mats are stable. You may have to place a support such as a chair against the outside of each mat. Have the children enter from a single starting point, but provide two or three ways to exit the maze. Use cones, hoops, and pillows to seal off parts of the maze and create various challenges.

To help children concentrate, play relaxing music as they try to find their way through the maze.

>>> Modifications

Make the maze more challenging by creating more intricate pathways. Ask the children to skip or hop through the maze.

Roman Candle .... Ages 4 to 6

››› *Objectives*

Catching and throwing skills

››› *Participants*

Four to six children

››› *Equipment and Materials*

Two folding mats, 10 to 15 foam balls

››› *Description*

Stand two folding mats on edge to form the "candle" and place the foam balls inside. Have one or two children stand inside the candle and the remaining children stand outside of it in a circle. At the "Go" signal, the children inside the candle begin tossing the foam balls outside of it. The children on the outside try to catch or chase the balls and toss them back in the candle. After 1 to 2 minutes, have the children change positions so that everyone gets a chance to be inside the candle.

››› *Modifications*

Use beanbags, beach balls, and stuffed animals if you need to supplement equipment.

Bocce Bowling . . . . Ages 4 to 6

≫ Objectives

Rolling, range

≫ Participants

2 to 12 children

≫ Equipment and Materials

Six **poly spots** (one for every two children), 12 baseball-sized **spider balls** or foam balls, 12 cones

≫ Description

Spread six poly spots throughout the play area and assign two tossers to each spot. Place two cones about 10 to 12 yards (9 to 11 meters) in front of the poly spots to mark the tossing line. The objective is for the children to get their spider ball as close to the poly spot as possible by rolling it from behind the tossing line.

Each child takes two turns, alternating with a friend. A child is allowed to knock out a friend's ball that is closer—it's part of the game. After four tosses, see which ball is closest to the poly spot. Then have the children start again and repeat the activity for several rounds, but do not keep score. To avoid confusion, you may want to assign a different color ball to each child.

≫ Modifications

Set up a plastic bowling pin in the center of the poly spot. The objective is to roll the ball as close to the pin as possible without knocking it over.

⫸ Objectives

Kicking skills

⫸ Participants

6 to 12 children

⫸ Equipment and Materials

One 6- to 8 1/2-inch- (15- to 22-centimeter-) diameter foam soccer ball per child, upbeat music, CD or tape player

⫸ Description

Start the music and instruct all children in the class to dribble (kick) a foam soccer ball around the play space using the inside of their foot. When the music stops, the children have to trap their ball by lightly stepping on it with the middle of their foot to stop it from rolling. Repeat the activity several times in 30-second intervals.

Next, ask half the children to stand erect with their legs spread wide apart. Restart the music and have the other half of the children begin to dribble around the open space. When they are within range (about 5 to 7 feet [1.5 to 2 meters]) of a child with open legs, they try to score a goal. Remind the children with open legs to allow the ball to pass through. After a few minutes, have the children change roles.

⫸ Modifications

This activity can be modified by having the children roll the ball through the goal (legs) when the music stops. Instead of having the children spread their legs, they can hold hoops upright at their sides to present a new goal challenge.

Cookie Jar . . . . Ages 4 to 6

>>> Objectives

Catching, throwing skills

>>> Participants

4 to 12 children

>>> Equipment and Materials

At least three foam balls or balls of different sizes for each child, small baskets for each child, rope

>>> Description

Divide the children into two groups. Suspend a rope about 4 feet (1.2 meters) above the surface of the play area, halfway between the two groups. The children all start with three balls in their baskets (cookie jars), which are positioned along the sideline of the play area. At the "Go" signal, all children run to their baskets, grab their balls, and start throwing them over the rope.

Both teams continue catching and throwing throughout the activity. The objective is to catch as many balls as possible that are thrown from the opposite side. When they make a catch, the children run to their basket to deposit the ball. After 2 minutes, repeat the activity from the start.

>>> Modifications

Follow up the activity with heart-healthy oatmeal cookies. Explain to the children that snacking on cookies is okay as long as they are healthy cookies. Ask the children to name other healthy snacks. Try to make the point that proper snacking and physical activity go hand in hand.

Partner Ball Carry . . . . Ages 4 to 6

>>> Objectives

Cooperation, body awareness

>>> Participants

2 to 12 children

>>> Equipment and Materials

Foam ball for each pair

>>> Description

Have the children find a partner and position themselves around the play area. Give each pair a foam ball. Next, begin calling out various body parts: elbows, knees, hands, backs. For example, when you call "Elbows!" the children must place the ball between each other's elbows and try to move as a pair while keeping the ball in place. Make a special point to emphasize that it takes cooperation to be successful. You may have to demonstrate how to secure the foam ball between partners.

>>> Modifications

Use different pieces of equipment such as beanbags, rubber rings, or stuffed animals.

Exploring Movement . . . . . . Ages 4 to 6

>>> Objectives

Personal and general space, pathways, levels, locomotor skills, creative movement

>>> Participants

1 to 12 children

>>> Equipment and Materials

One hoop per child, tambourine, whistle, drum

>>> Description

Scatter hoops throughout the play area. Ask the children to find their personal home by standing inside a hoop. Explain to the children that when you strike the tambourine twice, it means they are to stop, look, and listen for the next activity.

Use verbal cues to direct the children:

- "How small can you get in your home space?" "How tall?" "How wide?"
- "Let's see if you can walk around your hoop. Good! Now walk backward around your hoop." "Hop in and out of your hoop." "Skip around your hoop."
- "Now walk around the area, but don't step in the hoops. When you pass a friend, give them a big smile." "Now let's walk again, but this time when you hear a whistle blast, it means to change direction."
- "Let's all try to walk at a low level." "Can you walk as if your legs are made of rubber?" "How would you walk if your legs were as stiff as steel?"
- "Now try to walk to the beat of the drum—tap, tap, tap, tap." (Change tempo—fast, medium, slow.) "How would you walk if the drumbeat was loud and forceful?" "How about if it was soft and gentle?"
- "Okay, it's starting to rain, and we have to get back to our home hoops. Show me how you get back to your home space. Don't get wet!"
- "Now that you are standing in your home hoop, reach up and touch the sky." "Stretch, higher, higher, and touch the sun." "Now touch the stars."

>>> Modifications

Use play balls to enhance the activity. For example, have the children bounce the ball in and out of the hoop, dribble around the hoop, or dribble throughout the play area, avoiding the hoops.

Soccer Golf . . . . Ages 4 to 6

>>> Objectives
Kicking skills, accuracy, dribbling

>>> Participants
1 to 12 children

>>> Equipment and Materials
A tree, three pins, an open box, one large hoop, cones, a cardboard box, large cutout shapes (circle, triangle, square), a sheet, one foam ball for each child, two pieces of rope about 8 feet (2.5 meters) in length, a number for each hole

>>> Description
First, set up a Soccer Golf challenge course as follows:

Holes

1. Kicking through the goal (two cones spread 6 feet [2 meters] apart)
2. Kicking over three plastic pins set 2 feet (60 centimeters) apart
3. Kicking the ball and hitting the large oak tree
4. Kicking the ball through a large cutout (triangle, circle, or square) about 3 feet (90 centimeters) high
5. Kicking the ball into a large cardboard box (e.g., an appliance box) turned on its side

Position the holes around the open play space at least 20 yards (18 meters) apart. Have the children begin the course at different holes (no more than two children at each hole). At the "Go" signal, the children begin to dribble (kick) the foam ball over to their hole and complete the activity. Children may move on only when they have completed the activity at their hole.

Allow the children to dribble the ball directly in front of the target. Do not keep track of the number of kicks or the time it takes to complete the course. The children have great fun practicing their kicking skills—and all are winners!

>>> Modifications
Have the children toss smaller foam balls through the challenge course and call it Baseball Golf.

SUMMARY

Young children ages two through six are anxious to learn new skills. In fact, you will often be teaching a skill that a child has never tried before. This can be very exciting for the children and will help motivate them to be physically active on a daily basis.

This chapter has broken down skill development into movement concepts (space, effort, relationships) and looked at how they can be used in conjunction with the movement themes (locomotor, nonlocomotor, manipulative). Numerous practical skill activities were included to help you get started.

When children learn and develop skills at a young age, there is a greater chance they will grow into active adults, confident and comfortable with their physical abilities. They will also be more open to trying and learning new physical skills throughout their lives.

Chapter 8

RHYTHM
AND MOVEMENT

For many years, music education centered on the ability of children to play an instrument or sing. A love of and appreciation for music can be enhanced, however, when children use their bodies as musical instruments to explore various tempos and rhythms. This approach will also enhance creativity and self-expression and foster a fuller appreciation of music. Also, since music and rhythms are so motivating to young children, it is an excellent way to increase **physical activity** levels on a daily basis.

Dance and rhythm activities may develop basic **locomotor skills** such as walking, hopping, and jumping and **nonlocomotor skills** such as bending, twisting, and turning. Moreover, teaching a variety of dance and rhythmic activities is a great way to communicate cultural and ethnic awareness. For example, if you have children of Hispanic descent in your group, plan several Latin rhythm activities to make the children feel more comfortable in your school or play group. Try to include a wide array of cultures to give your activity selections variety and balance. Finally, when parents, teachers, or caregivers sing, dance, and move with young children, it helps create a special, personal bond that will have a lasting effect throughout the year.

RHYTHM AND MOVEMENT RECOMMENDATIONS

Some children may be reticent when you ask them to dance, sing, or be creative with rhythmic activity. But don't give up—children usually become more comfortable after a few introductory activities. To ensure a safe and positive learning experience, keep in mind the following five rhythm and movement recommendations.

1. Start with slow, controlled movements and progress from simple to more advanced movements.
2. An activity should consist of approximately 1- to 2-minute movement segments with intermittent rest periods throughout.
3. To avoid overuse strains, do not repeat a movement more than four consecutive times on one leg. Also, avoid unsupported forward trunk flexion, which can place stress on the lower back (see appendix C for other **contraindicated exercises**).
4. Ensure that children maintain proper posture and body alignment.
5. If possible, have children remove their shoes to get a better feel for the movement. If this is not possible, they should wear standard sneakers and cotton socks.

As you plan rhythmic and movement activities for children, try to include the most popular children's music associated with animated characters. But don't forget to include classical music, the old standard Disney tunes, and traditional children's rhymes to round out your selection.

DEVELOPMENTAL STAGES OF MUSICAL EXPERIENCES

According to movement education specialist Rae Pica (2000), just as children go through different stages mentally, physically, and socially, they also go through the stages of musical development at their own pace. Included are examples of how music is experienced at different ages, although these may vary from child to child.

Two-Year-Olds

- Respond to music, often by bouncing up and down
- Can learn short, simple songs
- Show the ability to follow directions in songs
- Respond to favorite songs, often asking to hear them repeatedly
- May sing parts of songs, but seldom sing with a group
- Enjoy experimenting with sounds, using objects for musical instruments
- Can discriminate among songs

Three-Year-Olds

- Have greater rhythmic ability
- Can recognize and sing parts of familiar tunes
- Make up their own songs
- Enjoy dramatizing songs

Four-Year-Olds

- Can grasp basic musical concepts such as tempo, volume, and pitch
- Show a dramatic increase in vocal range and rhythmic ability
- Create new lyrics for songs
- Enjoy more complex songs
- Love silly songs
- Prefer "active" listening (singing, moving, doing fingerplays, accompanying music with instruments)

Five- to Six-Year-Olds

- Can reproduce a melody
- Begin to synchronize movements with the music's rhythm
- Enjoy singing and moving with a group
- Have established musical preferences
- Can perform two movements simultaneously (e.g., marching and playing a rhythm instrument)

The following rhythm and movement activities include a variety of experiences for children that are easy to incorporate and will help you get started right away. Many require little space and limited equipment. Several rhythmic activities are ideal for the typical 10-minute break in the day that children and adults often need.

Eentsy Weentsy . . . . Ages 2 to 3

>>> Objectives

Self-expression, increase physical activity levels

>>> Participants

1 to 12 children

>>> Equipment and Materials

Large mat or carpeted area

>>> Description

Have the children scatter throughout the play area. Sing the traditional melody of "Eentsy Weentsy Spider."

Oh, the eentsy weentsy spider

Went up the water spout.

(children are on the floor on hands and feet doing crawling movements)

Down came the rain

And washed the spider out.

(children flatten out and perform a log roll)

Out came the sun

And dried up all the rain.

(children stand up and reach for the sky with both hands)

And the eentsy weentsy spider

Went up the spout again.

(children repeat the first movement)

>>> Modifications

As an alternative for young children, have them use fingers to imitate the spider movements.

Pop Goes the Weasel . . . . . . Ages 2 to 3

>>> Objectives

Group dancing, jumping, levels, tempo

>>> Participants

3 to 12 children

>>> Equipment and Materials

Music: "Pop! Goes the Weasel"; CD or tape player

>>> Description

Have the children form a circle and hold hands. Vary the movements, levels, and tempo to make this old standard new and exciting. First, ask the children to get low and begin to sing along with you or the recording:

Round and round the cobbler's bench

The monkey chased the weasel,

(children stay low)

In and out and round about singing

Pop! goes the weasel.

(children jump upward on the "Pop!")

Next, have the children walk together in a circle holding hands.

Round and round the cobbler's bench

The monkey chased the weasel,

(children walk in a circle)

In and out and round about singing

(children walk to the center of the circle)

Pop! goes the weasel.

(children jump upward on the "Pop!")

>>> Modifications

Instead of the children jumping up on the "Pop!" sound, have them "freeze" and then continue moving when the song resumes.

Wiggle Workout . . . . Ages 2 to 3

>>> Objectives
Nonlocomotor skills, levels, body part identification

>>> Participants
1 to 12 children

>>> Equipment and Materials
Song: "Wiggle, Wiggle, Shake & Giggle"

>>> Description
Have the children sit in a circle. Begin exploring different body parts by asking the children to wiggle them on the following cues:

- "Hands"
- "Hands up high"
- "Hands to your sides"
- "Feet"
- "Feet up high" (children lean back with their feet in the air)
- "Nose"
- "Tongue"
- "Shoulders"

Try using the song "Wiggle, Wiggle, Shake & Giggle" (lyrics as follows):

Wiggle like a worm
Wiggle like a snake
Then wind it up
And shake, shake, shake!
Wiggle a little
Now wiggle a lot
Then stay right there
And shake in your spot!
Let's see a wiggle
Let's see a shake
Now it's time to
Take a giggle break!

From Moving and Learning Series: Preschoolers & Kindergartners 1st edition by PICA/GARDZINA, © 2000. Reprinted with permission of Delmar Learning, a division of Thomson Learning: www.thomsonrights.com. Fax 800-730-2215.

>>> Modifications
Play upbeat children's music and provide your own directions to wiggle and shake various body parts.

Here We Go Round the Mulberry Bush .... Ages 2 to 6

»» *Objectives*

Expressive rhythmic movement, increase physical activity levels

»» *Participants*

2 to 12 children

»» *Equipment and Materials*

Large plastic pot, crepe paper

»» *Description*

Place a large plastic pot filled with colored crepe paper in the middle of a circle. Drape strips of paper over the edge to replicate a bush. Have the children form a circle around the plastic pot (mulberry bush) and begin walking around the circle and chanting:

> Here we go round the mulberry bush,
> Mulberry bush, mulberry bush.
> Here we go round the mulberry bush
> On a cold and frosty morning.
> (Change lyrics for the next four verses, but use the same melody.)
> This is how we wash our clothes,
> Wash our clothes, wash our clothes.
> This is how we wash our clothes
> (children continue to walk in a circle and pretend to scrub clothes)
> On a cold and frosty morning.
> This is how we march to school,
> March to school, march to school.
> This is how we march to school
> (children march step around the circle)
> On a cold and frosty morning.
> This is how we stretch so high,
> Stretch so high, stretch so high.
> This is how we stretch so high
> (children stop and reach both hands straight overhead)
> On a cold and frosty morning.

This is how we jog on home,
Jog on home, jog on home.
This is how we jog on home
(children jog slowly around the circle)
On a cold and frosty morning.

››› Modifications

Think of different chants to vary the locomotor movements.

≫ Objectives

Physical imitation, visual interpretation, attention skills

≫ Participants

1 to 12 children

≫ Equipment and Materials

Music: "Moving to Mozart" or any classical music with a steady rhythm; CD or tape player; scarves (one for each child)

≫ Description

Have the children scatter throughout the play area. Stand directly in front of the children so that everyone can easily see your entire body. Explain to the children that they will pretend to be in front of a large mirror trying to imitate the exact movements you are going to perform. Begin the following movements without music.

- Make a big smile.
- Lift your shoulders to your ears and lower them.
- Circle your shoulders backward.
- Raise your eyebrows high and lower them.
- Move your waist from side to side.

Next, play classical music and change the movements to match the tempo.

- Raise both arms overhead.
- Stretch your arms out like the wings of a bird.
- Lift your left knee and lower it, then raise your right knee and lower it.
- Get real low.
- Raise up high on your toes.

Finally, pass out the colored scarves.

- Wave the scarf up and down with one hand.
- Circle it around your head.
- Cross it in front of your body in a figure X.
- Toss it up and catch it.
- Wave it like a flag and walk around the play area.

⋙ *Modifications*

Four- to six-year-olds can be grouped in pairs. Ask one child to lead first and perform any movements; the follower has to shadow the movements. After several minutes, have the children change roles. The leader can also include various locomotor skills such as hopping, walking like a duck, or moving like a monkey.

The Tightrope Dance . . . . . . Ages 2 to 6

››› Objectives

Balance, rhythmic movement to music, levels, pathways

››› Participants

2 to 12 children

››› Equipment and Materials

Colored gym tape or jump ropes, classical music with a slow tempo, CD or tape player

››› Description

Have the children spread out in the play area. Mark lines on the floor, about 6 to 8 feet (2 to 2.5 meters) in length, using gym tape or rope; allow at least one for each child. Give the lines different shapes: curved, zigzag, L-shaped, and so on. Start the music and direct the children to find a line on the floor and begin walking to the classical music. When the music stops, all children "freeze" on their lines. Repeat the activity several times, changing the movement and having the children change lines each time. Use the following verbal cues:

- "Walk on your line, as low as you can go." (change the tempo slightly)
- "Walk sideways on your line."
- "Walk backward on your line."
- "Hop on your line." (change the tempo to upbeat music)
- "Jog on the line on the floor. Go from one line to another and move around the play area."

››› Modifications

Add different locomotor skills to the activity.

Row, Row, Row Your Boat . . . Ages 2 to 6

>>> Objectives

Expressive rhythmic movement, increase physical activity levels

>>> Participants

1 to 12 children

>>> Equipment and Materials

Two **streamers** per child, two carpet squares per child (optional)

>>> Description

Ask the children to spread themselves throughout the play area. Explain to them that they are pretending to spend a day on the lake. Some activities will be in the summer when it is nice and warm. Other activities will be in the winter when the lake is frozen.

Begin in the summer, on a bright, sunny day. Pass out two streamers per child.

Lead the group in chanting:

Row, row, row your boat

Gently down the stream.

(children walk around pretending to row a boat with both arms, one streamer in each hand)

Merrily, merrily, merrily, merrily,

Life is but a dream.

Row, row, row your boat

Quickly down the stream.

(children jog and row faster with both arms)

Merrily, merrily, merrily, merrily,

Life is but a dream.

Swim, swim, swim yourself

Gently down the stream.

(children jog around the area using the front crawl swim stroke with streamers in hand)

Merrily, merrily, merrily, merrily,

Life is but a dream.

Fish, fish, fish for fish

Gently down the stream.

(children pretend to use the streamers as fishing rods, casting outward from overhead)

Merrily, merrily, merrily, merrily,

Life is but a dream.

Use the following verbal cues:

> "Okay, now it's January—the winter—and the lake is frozen. Brrr! Everyone put on their coats, hats, and gloves."
>
> (children make believe they are putting on warm clothing; pass out two carpet squares for each child)
>
> Skate, skate, skate yourself
>
> Gently down the stream.
>
> (children pretend that each carpet square is a skate)
>
> Merrily, merrily, merrily, merrily,
>
> Life is but a dream.

≫ Modifications

Include additional movements by having the children pretend to perform other activities on the lake. Paper plates can be substituted for carpet squares.

Freeze Dance . . . . Ages 2 to 6

>>> Objectives

Self-expression, increase physical activity levels, listening skills

>>> Participants

2 to 12 children

>>> Equipment and Materials

Mix of various music: rock and roll, march music, children's tunes, waltz music; CD or tape player

>>> Description

Design a mix of music on one CD. Ask the children to spread out in the open space. Instruct them to move any way they would like, expressing themselves by moving to the music. When you stop the music, they must freeze like statues.

Vary the pattern of stopping the music (e.g., after 5 seconds, 10 seconds, 15 seconds, 5 seconds, 5 seconds, 15 seconds).

This activity will expose children to a variety of music and rhythms, as well as allow them to create and express individual movement patterns.

>>> Modifications

Provide each child with various pieces of equipment such as scarves, streamers, play balls, and beanbags. Ask the children to move to the music while manipulating the object.

This Old Man . . . . Ages 2 to 6

»» *Objectives*

Rhythmic movement with chanting, counting skills, **warm-up** activity

»» *Participants*

1 to 12 children

»» *Equipment and Materials*

None

»» *Description*

Have the children scatter throughout the play area, spacing themselves at least 3 feet (1 meter) apart. Lead the group through a series of rhythmic movements while chanting the song "This Old Man."

> This old man, he played one
> He played nick nack on my drum
> (children imitate beating on a drum)
> With a nick nack, paddy whack give a dog a bone
> (children imitate a dog barking: "ruff, ruff")
> This old man came rolling home.
> (children make fists and roll their hands)
> This old man, he played two
> He played nick nack on my shoe
> (children stomp their feet)
> With a nick nack, paddy whack give a dog a bone
> (children imitate a dog barking: "ruff, ruff")
> This old man came rolling home.
> (children make fists and roll their hands)
> This old man, he played three
> He played nick nack on my knee
> (children tap their knees)
> With a nick nack, paddy whack give a dog a bone
> (children imitate a dog barking: "ruff, ruff")
> This old man came rolling home.
> (children make fists and roll their hands)

This old man, he played four

He played nick nack on my door

(children imitate knocking on a door)

With a nick nack, paddy whack give a dog a bone

(children imitate a dog barking: "ruff, ruff")

This old man came rolling home.

(children make fists and roll their hands)

This old man, he played five

He played nick nack with some jive

(children alternate their fists up and down, arms extended in front of them)

With a nick nack, paddy whack give a dog a bone

(children imitate a dog barking: "ruff, ruff")

This old man came rolling home.

(children make fists and roll their hands)

≫ *Modifications*

Keep counting and create additional movements for the five- and six-year-olds: six— "with my sticks," seven—"up in heaven," eight —"on my skates," and so on.

If You're Happy and You Know It .... Ages 2 to 6

>>> Objectives

Rhythmic movements with chanting, increase physical activity levels

>>> Participants

1 to 12 children

>>> Equipment and Materials

None

>>> Description

Have the children scatter throughout the play area. Lead the group in a series of rhythmic movements while chanting the song "If You're Happy and You Know It."

> If you're happy and you know it, clap your hands (clap, clap)
> If you're happy and you know it, clap your hands (clap, clap)
> If you're happy and you know it and you really want to show it
> If you're happy and you know it, clap your hands. (clap, clap)
> If you're happy and you know it, stomp your feet (stomp, stomp)
> If you're happy and you know it, stomp your feet (stomp, stomp)
> If you're happy and you know it and you really want to show it
> If you're happy and you know it, stomp your feet. (stomp, stomp)
> If you're happy and you know it, jump up and down (jump, jump)
> If you're happy and you know it, jump up and down (jump, jump)
> If you're happy and you know it and you really want to show it
> If you're happy and you know it, jump up and down. (jump, jump)
> If you're happy and you know it, walk and laugh ("ha, ha")
> If you're happy and you know it, walk and laugh ("ha, ha")
> If you're happy and you know it and you really want to show it
> If you're happy and you know it, walk and laugh. ("ha, ha")

>>> Modifications

Have the children perform additional movements such as patting their knees, touching their head, and so on, or express different feelings such as acting surprised, acting scared, and the like.

Old MacDonald Had a Healthy Body . . . . Ages 2 to 6

>>> Objectives

Body part identification, reinforcing healthy bodies, warm-up activity

>>> Participants

1 to 12 children

>>> Equipment and Materials

None

>>> Description

Arrange the children in a circle, facing the center. Lead the group in chanting the old standard melody of "Old MacDonald Had a Farm," but use different lyrics for this activity to help reinforce a healthy body. For example, during the verse about healthy arms, the children bend their arms to the rhythm of the chant.

> Old MacDonald had a healthy body, E-I-E-I-O
> And on his body he had healthy arms, E-I-E-I-O
> With a bend-bend here and a bend-bend there
> Here a bend, there a bend
> Everywhere a bend-bend
> Old MacDonald had healthy arms, E-I-E-I-O.
> Old MacDonald had a healthy body, E-I-E-I-O
> And on his body he had healthy legs, E-I-E-I-O
> With a march-march here and a march-march there
> Here a march, there a march
> Everywhere a march-march
> Old MacDonald had healthy legs, E-I-E-I-O.
> Old MacDonald had a healthy body, E-I-E-I-O
> And on his body he had a healthy heart, E-I-E-I-O
> With a jog-jog here and a jog-jog there
> Here a jog, there a jog,
> Everywhere a jog-jog
> Old MacDonald had a healthy heart, E-I-E-I-O.

>>> Modifications

Change body parts and add different locomotor movements. Make straw farmer hats for each child, and have them perform for the parents or other children.

>>> Objectives

Self-expression to music, imagination, balance, increase physical activity levels

>>> Participants

1 to 12 children

>>> Equipment and Materials

Music: "Surfin' U.S.A." (The Beach Boys, Capitol Records); CD or tape player; one carpet section for each child

>>> Description

Ask the children to scatter throughout the play area and stand on their carpet squares. Explain that the carpet squares will be their surfboards. If the children are not familiar with surfing, show them pictures or a short video of surfers moving across the waves. Help out by participating in and leading the activity using a series of verbal cues.

- "Let's wax down your surfboard."
- "Place your hand on the board on the floor, lie down on your stomach, and swim out to the waves. Kick your legs."
- "Hop on top of your surfboard . . . balance yourself, knees bent, feet apart!"
- "Lean to the right . . . don't fall off!"
- "Lean to the left."
- "Surf on one leg . . . now the other."
- "Twist your surfboard to change directions."
- "Get real low . . . bend your knees."
- "Stand up tall on your surfboard."
- "Now hop off your board and swim around the play area. Do a front crawl (arms move forward), a backstroke (arms move backward), and a breaststroke (left arm moves to the left, right arm moves to the right—stroke from chest level)."
- "Finish by jumping up and down in the water. 'Everybody's been surfin', surfin' U.S.A.!'"

≫ *Modifications*

Have the children make their own surfboards out of cardboard, or have the boards already cut out and ask the children to decorate and color them. Now you're ready to go surfing!

The Beat Goes On . . . . Ages 2 to 6

>>> *Objectives*

Tempo, force, self-expression, locomotor skills

>>> *Participants*

2 to 12 children

>>> *Equipment and Materials*

One standard drum, one drumstick

>>> *Description*

Explain to the children that they will be moving to the beat of the drum. Each drumbeat will represent a step. Ask the children to spread out and find their personal space. Here are some suggested activities:

1. Beat the drum hard in an even four count: 1-2-3-4.
2. Tap the drum lightly in an even four count: 1-2-3-4.
3. Beat the drum in an even four count with 1-2 (hard) and 3-4 (light).
4. Beat the drum slowly: 1-rest-2-rest-3-rest-4-rest.
5. Beat the drum in a fast, even beat.
6. Beat the drum in uneven beats: 1-2, 1-2, 1-2, 1-2.
7. Make various angular movements by bending your arms and hands in different shapes to a four-count beat: 1-2-3-4. (Alternatives: Have the children try doing this with one leg; ask them to lie down and use both legs.)
8. Try different locomotor skills such as jogging to the beat, walking, marching, or crawling.

>>> *Modifications*

Try using different instruments instead of the drum, such as a tambourine, **lummi sticks**, a wood block, or a drumstick.

>>> Objectives

Locomotor movements, creative expression, balance

>>> Participants

3 to 12 children

>>> Equipment and Materials

Circus music, CD or tape player, top hat, streamer, scarves (one or two for each child), pictures of various circus animals or performers

>>> Description

Have the children scatter themselves around the play area. Explain to them that they will pretend they are all going to the circus! You will be the ring leader with top hat and streamer. As you give the verbal cue for each circus act, hold up a picture of the animal or performer you're asking the children to imitate.

- "First, let's pretend we are tightrope walkers. Everyone find a line on the floor. Try to stay on the lines—don't fall off!" (If no lines are available, use colored tape to establish 4- to 6-foot [1- to 2-meter] lines around the play area.)
- "Now, let's make believe we are horses galloping around the circus in a great big circle."
- "Okay, it's time for the clowns to come out. Let's all be funny clowns. How do clowns act? How do they move?"
- "Now we are all monkeys. Show me how a monkey moves. How do they act?"
- "Oh, oh! Here come the tigers! Everyone get down and move like a tiger. How does a tiger sound?"
- "It's time for the juggling clowns. Make believe you are a funny clown trying to juggle the colorful scarves. Try not to let the scarves touch the floor!"
- "What great circus acts! Everyone clap and cheer. Now take a bow."

>>> Modifications

Provide various circus pictures and ask the children to color them. Design a circus routine with different children acting out various roles.

>>> Objectives

Tempo and movement, cooperation

>>> Participants

2 to 12 children

>>> Equipment and Materials

Lummi sticks (optional)

>>> Description

Arrange the children in small groups of two or three. Ask each group to sit down in a straight line, one behind the other. In this formation, practice the rhythmic chant and movements before the train pulls out of the station:

- Clap, clap
- Tap, tap (knees)
- "Whoo-whoo" (pull the whistle)

Remind the children that the line leader is the locomotive and must give direction to the rest of the train when it pulls out to start the journey. Begin the activity by starting the chant. Everyone stands up, and the leader begins walking around the play area. After about a minute, stop the train and change the locomotive (leader).

>>> Modifications

Provide each child with two lummi sticks and change the chant as follows: two clicks of the sticks high together, two clicks of the sticks low together, "whoo-whoo."

Hokey Pokey . . . . Ages 4 to 6

>>> Objectives

Locomotor skills, body part identification, group dance

>>> Participants

4 to 12 children

>>> Equipment and Materials

Music: "Hokey Pokey"; CD or tape player

>>> Description

Arrange children in a large circle facing the center. Practice chanting the lyrics and performing the movements before playing the song. When you feel the children have grasped the movements and patterns, you can begin the activity.

Have the children start by walking slowly in a circle, then stop to sing the song. Begin by putting the right hand in, and then change the verse to different body parts: right leg, right hip, head, whole body, and so on. At the end of the song, have everyone clap their hands to the last line: "That's what it's all about!" Everyone cheer!

>>> Modifications

Instead of moving various body parts, have the children manipulate various pieces of equipment such as scarves, streamers, and beanbags.

>>> Objectives

Rhythmic expressive movement, manipulative skills

>>> Participants

1 to 2 children

>>> Equipment and Materials

Music: "Wheels on the Bus"; two streamers per child

>>> Description

Arrange the children in a circle, at least 3 feet (1 meter) apart, each holding a streamer in their right hand. *Note:* Streamers can be made by starting with an aluminum wrap or paper towel core to use as the handle. Wrap crepe paper around the handle and tape it securely. Next, cut three or four pieces of crepe paper about 3 feet (1 meter) long. Tape the ends of the crepe paper pieces to the top of the handle, allowing them to fall freely.

Have the children walk in a circle while circling the streamer in front of them. Then start the first verse of the song:

> The wheels on the bus go round and round,
> Round and round, round and round.
> (all children circle the streamer on their right side)
> The wheels on the bus go round and round,
> All through the town.
> (all children stop)
> The wipers on the bus go *swish, swish, swish,*
> *Swish, swish, swish, swish, swish, swish.*
> The wipers on the bus go *swish, swish, swish,*
> All through the town.
> (all children wave their streamer back and forth in front of their body)
> The driver on the bus goes "Move on back!
> Move on back, move on back!"
> The driver on the bus goes "Move on back!"
> All through the town.
> (all children raise the streamer overhead and move it backward on the words "Move on back")
> The horn on the bus goes *beep, beep, beep,*
> *Beep, beep, beep, beep, beep, beep.*

The horn on the bus goes *beep, beep, beep,*

All through the town.

(all children move the streamer in a quick, forceful downward
  movement from waist level as they recite each "beep")

End by repeating the first verse with the children again walking in a circle
and circling the streamer in front of them.

⋙ *Modifications*

Use hand movements instead of streamers.

Dance Down the Lines . . . . . Ages 4 to 6

>>> *Objectives*

Self-expression, rhythmic movement, increase physical activity levels

>>> *Participants*

6 to 12 children

>>> *Equipment and Materials*

Upbeat children's music, CD or tape player

>>> *Description*

Arrange the children in two lines facing each other. Designate the beginning of both lines. Explain to the children that they will all be dancing together, but they will have the opportunity to dance down the lines and create any movements they would like to the beat of the music.

First, have the children at the beginning of each line take their turn dancing down the line and then return to the end of the same line. The children in the lines march in place while moving their arms to the music and slowly move sideways toward the beginning of the line.

Next, ask the two children who are now at the beginning of the line to join hands and dance together down the line, then return to the end of the same line. Continue until all children have had a chance to dance down the line.

>>> *Modifications*

Change the movements for the children in the lines; vary the music; use themes such as swim music, walking music, or marching music.

SUMMARY

Children love to sing, dance, and move rhythmically. Take advantage of this interest to help them appreciate the joy of music and movement and how it can also help them stay fit and healthy throughout their lives. Visit the children's section of educational supply stores and major retailers to keep up to date on new music and activity CDs. Popular children's TV characters are often used to help motivate dance and rhythm activity, but don't forget the old standards that have held up over time.

This chapter provided a sampling of traditional chanting activities (Old MacDonald Had a Healthy Body), as well as more contemporary choices (Wiggle Workout). Try to incorporate rhythm and movement into a child's day; it will not only add variety to your program but also will be a motivating change of pace and will keep children excited about physical activity.

YOGA FOR KIDS

Since the early 1990s, parents, teachers, and caregivers have become increasingly aware of the benefits of yoga for kids. The word *yoga* means "union"—the union that occurs between the mind and body, creating a personal sense of balance and harmony. Yoga is an excellent physical activity for children ages two through six because it is noncompetitive and promotes self-expression through movement. It also enhances attention span, concentration skills, and body awareness. In our fast-paced, stressful lifestyle, yoga has become popular as a way to slow down, relax, and enjoy quality quiet time. Yoga enables adults as well as children to recenter their energy and reflect on their lives on a daily basis. From a physical perspective, yoga is beneficial in promoting balance, stability, strength, coordination, **flexibility**, and **nonlocomotor skills.**

Yoga was originally developed around a series of poses imitating animals. The notion was that if people did the same exercises and performed the same movements as animals, they too would be strong, flexible, and healthy. More recently, yoga has advanced to include numerous interpretations. Try to design your own or have the children help you create different images. Provide them with pictures of poses, such as a mad cat, a mountain range, a tree, and the like, to create a visual image that they can imitate.

Caution!

Many of the poses found in popular books on yoga and yoga for children include **contraindicated exercises** or movements that may have harmful effects. Some yoga movements place undue stress on the neck, back, and other major joints such as the knee (see appendix C).

HELPFUL HINTS

Keep in mind the following helpful hints for making yoga a positive experience for young children.

1. All poses should be performed using slow, controlled movements. Each pose should be held for several seconds, or as long as the children feel comfortable.

2. Encourage children to relax, breathe slowly, and think positively. Use background music.

3. Make sure children do not force the movements or go beyond their individual limitations.

4. Never compare children—some may be more flexible than others. Continued practice will make the movements easier. Remember, all pose interpretations are correct.

5. Yoga should be performed on a mat or carpeted surface, and children should remove their shoes. They should also avoid eating for at least an hour before performing yoga movements to help settle or calm the entire body.

The following poses are arranged starting with breathing exercises and then in order of body positioning—standing, kneeling, sitting, lying—and finally support movements. The last section describes a few games that may add some fun and excitement to yoga activities.

BREATHING POSES

The following poses center on breathing to help regulate the heart rate and bring the body into balance.

Candle

Have the children sit with their legs folded and in good posture, with their chin slightly lowered and their shoulders and neck relaxed. Next, have them adopt the pose by raising their hands to head level with their fingers spread, pointing up. Tell the children to pretend that their hands are a candle and their fingers are the flame. Have them close their eyes, take in one deep breath, and gently release it by bringing their arms down slowly. They should continue to breathe evenly for 1 to 2 minutes and stay very quiet, with their hands resting on their legs. Ask the children to think of something they like and why it makes them happy.

Balloon Breathing

Have the children lie on their back and relax. Ask them to pretend that there is a balloon on their stomach, and when they breathe in, the balloon is slowly filling their stomach with air. When they breathe out, the balloon empties and their stomach flattens out. Try placing a balloon on each child's stomach and have them practice slow, relaxed stomach breathing. Ask the children to control the balloon on their stomach with controlled breathing.

STANDING POSES

The following poses are performed from a standing posture, which will enhance balance and body symmetry.

Tree

From a standing position, the children should bend their right knee outward and lift upward. Next, have them slide their right foot into their inner thigh and gently rest it in that position. Then have them raise their arms out to the sides to imitate the branches of a tree. After reaching stability, they should raise both arms straight overhead to represent high-level branches.

Younger children may have more success by crossing one leg in front of their support leg in the junior tree pose.

Mountain

Instruct the children to stand as tall and straight as they can, keeping their feet firmly on the ground. Ask them to pretend their shoulders are the mountaintop and their head is the peak of the mountain. They should keep their arms at their sides and point their fingers straight at the ground. Have them take in a deep breath and then breathe out and relax. Tell them to stand very still and very straight—just like a mountain.

Hero

Have the children stand with their feet spread wide apart. Instruct them to turn their left foot toward their left side, slightly bending the knee and turning their body in that direction (the knee should not move past the left foot). Then have them raise both arms out to their sides, hold, then change to the opposite side.

Bird

Have the children stand with their arms at their sides and raise both arms backward with the palms facing up toward the sky. Then have them rise up onto their toes, keeping their head up, and pretend they are a bird flying through the air. Instruct them to look straight ahead and focus on an object, then balance and hold.

KNEELING POSES

The following poses are performed from a kneeling position to enhance balance using various body parts at a low level.

Cat

Have the children begin on their hands and knees. Ask them to gently round their upper back while tightening and tucking their stomach muscles. Then have them slowly lower their head, keeping their back and shoulders relaxed.

Camel

Starting from the cat position, the children should gently relax their back and flatten out, keeping their back straight. They should then arch their back slightly by relaxing their lower back, lifting their chin, and gently pressing their stomach into the floor.

197

Squirrel

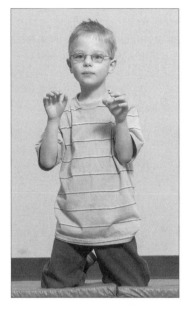

Instruct the children to begin by sitting back on their heels and then slowly raising up to a kneeling position. Next, have them bend both arms and bring their hands up just beneath their chin, with the palms facing outward and the fingers cupped. Ask them to hold and then slowly repeat the movement.

Ostrich

From a starting position on their hands and knees, have the children place their hands in front of them, about shoulder-width apart. The palms should be flat and facing inward with the fingers pointing toward each other. Instruct the children to keep their knees together. Next, have them slightly bend their elbows and lean forward. Then tell them to lift both feet while keeping their knees on the floor and their head and back straight. Have them hold the pose, release by slowly sitting back on their heels, and then repeat the movement.

SITTING POSES

The following poses are performed from a sitting position to enhance stability and creativity.

Star

Ask the children to sit with their knees bent and the soles of their feet together. Have them overlap their fingers behind their head and point their elbows out to the sides. Make sure they maintain good posture.

Flower

Have the children begin by sitting with the soles of their feet together. Instruct them to slowly bring one arm at a time underneath their lower legs (left arm under the left leg and right arm under the right leg) and gently hold the front of their shins. Next, have them slowly straighten their back and keep their head up, hold, then release one arm at a time.

Bouquet of Flowers

Arrange three to five children in a circle, sitting close together. Begin by having them practice the flower pose. Remind the children that a group of flowers is called a bouquet. Next, have them raise their legs and slowly lean back, then grasp hands with the children on either side of them—their left hand grasping the right hand of the child on their left and their right hand grasping the left hand of the child on their right—between their legs. Tell them to lean back and relax with their head up so that the entire group can balance.

Modification: You can tie a large rope in a circle for the children to hold onto so they can lean back with their legs up and stay balanced.

Peacock

Have the children begin from a sitting position and straighten their legs outward as far as possible. Instruct them to point their toes straight up and keep their back straight. Next, have them place their hands on the floor in front of them, close to their body, with the palms down. Then have them press downward gently to widen their shoulders.

LYING POSES

The following poses are performed from a lying position to enhance low-level activity as well as concentration and stability.

Cloud

Have the children lie flat on the carpet or mat, facing up, with their hands at their sides. Their arms and legs should be spread wide apart. Remind the children to relax (eyes may be open or closed) and stay calm and quiet. Ask them to pretend they are a cloud floating in the sky as you say the following: "Your body is very light as it moves around the sky. You are floating in the air, feeling very happy and relaxed." Then have the children take a deep breath and exhale slowly.

Starfish

Direct the children to lie flat on the carpet or mat, facing up, with their eyes closed. Then have them spread their legs as wide as feels comfortable and spread their arms out to the sides with the palms either facing up or facing down while resting on the mat. Ask them to pretend they are a starfish, floating on the water in the ocean, as you say the following in a soothing voice: "Feel the waves move you gently up, down, and around. Relax and breathe quietly. Now you have reached the shore." Then have them slowly bring their legs and arms in and gently roll themselves up.

Modified Cobra

Ask the children to lie on their stomach with their legs together and straight. Have them place their palms down on the mat and rest on their elbows, keeping their hands close to their chest. Then have them raise their chest, keeping their shoulders straight and wide. They should try to keep their head up and their neck long and straight. (*Note:* Do not allow children to arch their neck backward.)

SUPPORT POSES

The following poses are performed in various support postures to enhance balance and stability.

Rainbow

Ask the children to lie on their left side, supporting their body with only their left arm. Instruct them to keep the arm straight and stable with the fingers spread slightly apart and keep both legs together with the right foot on top. Then have them gently swing their right arm up to the sky as you tell them: "You're a rainbow—full of color and beauty." This pose is more suitable for children ages four to six.

Table

Have the children begin in a seated position with their knees bent and their feet flat on the floor, about 3 inches (8 centimeters) apart. Next, ask them to place their hands several inches (centimeters) behind them, fingers pointing toward their feet. Then have them press their hands and feet into the floor and lift their hips, making their stomach as flat as possible. Ask them to hold the position and then release gently.

GAMES

The following games help bring the yoga poses to life and add fun and social interaction to the learning experience.

Frozen Yoga

Play background music and instruct the children to move in various ways throughout the play area. After 30 seconds or so, stop the music and call out a yoga pose (e.g., "Tree!"). The children must all stop what they are doing and pose like a tree. Start the music again and call out a different pose (e.g., "Cobra!"), and continue on in that manner.

Growing Flowers

Ask the children to form a circle. Explain that everyone will become a small seed that will be planted in the early spring, and by the middle of summer the seed will become a beautiful flower. Then ask the children to make themselves as small as possible, just like a flower seed (show them an example of a flower seed to reinforce how small they are). Instruct the children to kneel down and sit back on their feet with their forehead on the ground, keeping their arms bent and close to their knees.

Ask the children to imagine they are a flower seed as you say the following in a soft voice: "As the weather gets warmer, you slowly lift your head. Then the sun gets even warmer and you start to rise, higher and higher. Now the spring turns to summer and you rise from your knees while sitting back on your heels. Open your arms from the side, then gently raise your arms overhead. Now slowly stand up as your arms greet the sun. Stand straight and tall and stretch as high as you can—reach for the sun and breathe in. Now lower your arms and breathe out. Think of a beautiful flower that you enjoy." Repeat the activity.

Posing Pictures

With a small group of children (three or four), have each child, one at a time, select a yoga pose from a bag or box and demonstrate it. The others must try to guess the name of the animal or the yoga pose.

SUMMARY

Yoga can be an excellent addition to your physical activity program. Use the yoga poses throughout the day to help your children create a mind-body relationship. The poses will also help relieve stress and teach children how to concentrate. Carefully follow the directions for each movement as described in this chapter, being mindful of correct body alignment and proper breathing techniques. The poses will help develop balance, stability, strength, coordination, flexibility, and nonlocomotor skills—but go slowly and give the children time to master and control each pose before adding another to a routine.

For more information on yoga, see appendix A (professional organizations) and appendix B (Web site resources).

Appendix A
Professional Organizations

American Academy of Pediatrics
141 Northwest Point Blvd.
Elk Grove Village, IL 60007-1098
847-434-4000
www.aap.org

American Alliance for Health, Physical Education, Recreation and Dance
1900 Association Dr.
Reston, VA 20191-1598
703-476-3400
www.aahperd.org

American Alliance for Health, Physical Education, Recreation and Dance Publications
P.O. Box 385
Oxon Hill, MD 20750-0385
800-321-0789
www.aahperd.org/naspe

American College of Sports Medicine
P.O. Box 1440
Indianapolis, IN 46206-1440
317-637-9200
www.acsm.org

American Council on Exercise

4851 Paramount Dr.
San Diego, CA 92123
800-825-3636
858-279-8227
www.acefitness.org

American Dietetic Association

120 South Riverside Plaza, Ste. 2000
Chicago, IL 60606-6995
800-877-1600
www.eatright.org

American Heart Association

National Center
7272 Greenville Ave.
Dallas, TX 75231
800-AHA-USA1
800-242-8721
www.amhrt.org

American Medical Association

515 N. State St.
Chicago, IL 60610
800-621-8335
www.ama-assn.org

American Public Health Association

800 I St. NW
Washington, DC 20001
202-777-2742
www.apha.org

American School Health Association

7263 State Rte. 43
P.O. Box 708
Kent, OH 44240
330-678-1601
www.ashaweb.org

Centers for Disease Control and Prevention

1600 Clifton Rd.
Atlanta, GA 30333
404-639-3311
www.cdc.gov

Food and Drug Administration

5600 Fishers Lane
Rockville, MD 20857-0001
800-216-7331
www.fda.gov

National Association for the Education of Young Children

1509 16th St. NW
Washington, DC 20036
202-232-8777
www.naeyc.org

National Institutes of Health

9000 Rockville Pike
Bethesda, MD 20892
www.nih.gov

The President's Council on Physical Fitness and Sports

Department W
200 Independence Ave. SW, Rm. 738-H
Washington, DC 20201-0004
202-690-9000
www.fitness.gov

U.S. Surgeon General's Office

The U.S. Department of Health & Human Services
200 Independence Ave. SW
Washington, DC 20201
202-619-0257
877-696-6775
www.surgeongeneral.gov/beinghealthy

Appendix B
Web Site Resources

www.aahperd.org/naspe/sportforall/

The Sport For All physical activity program for 3- to 10-year-olds is a joint partnership of NASPE, Human Kinetics, and Sportime. Site includes colorful content and activity cards for teachers.

www.bechoosy.org

University of West Virginia Motor Development Center for Young Children. Includes motor skills and physical activities for preschoolers.

www.dole5aday.com

Dole Food Company Web site. Includes great eating suggestions, educational activities, and recipes emphasizing fruits and vegetables.

www.health.gov/dietaryguidelines/dga2005/document

Seventy-page document developed by the USDA (*Dietary Guidelines for Americans* 2005). This document complements the MyPyramid diet recommendations.

www.healthfinder.gov

Healthfinder is a consumer resource developed by the federal government with many links to children's health topics.

www.hearteheart.com

Heart health curriculum for children. Includes cartoon characters to teach concepts about healthy eating and exercise.

www.HumanKinetics.com

Human Kinetics Inc., a leader in the production of educational books and materials in physical education, exercise, and sport.

www.just-for-kids.org

Information about a children's obesity prevention program as well as a variety of other topics for kids.

www.keepkidshealthy.com

Includes up-to-date nutrition ideas for children with ready-to-use recipes.

www.kidshealth.org

General site with multiple categories, including nutrition and physical activity.

www.kimboed.com

Kimbo Educational is an excellent children's music company offering great selections of physical activity music for young children such as Hap Palmer, Greg and Steve, Georgiana Stewart, and Raffi.

www.learningthroughsports.com

This site was developed to help educationally motivated students from 5 to 14 using sports-based activities in interactive educational software.

www.movingandlearning.com

Resources for young children. Includes books, CDs for motor skill development, music, and creative movement activities.

www.mypyramid.com

USDA Web site for the 2005 food pyramid.

www.parentalwisdom.com

Great site for parents. Includes interesting topics such as children's health, parenting strategies for behavior management, and a monthly question-and-answer section.

www.peacefulplaygrounds.com

Introduces children and school staff to the many choices available on playgrounds. Includes a program kit with more than 100 games and activities.

www.pecentral.com

Excellent Web site for health and physical education teachers. Includes all related topics: curriculum, fitness, assessment, and special physical education; also includes a section for Pre-K activities.

www.pe4life.org

PE4life promotes active, healthy lifestyles through physical education.

www.pelinks4u.org

One of the most popular Web sites in the world for physical education teachers. Includes lesson plans and activities for children geared to the physical education teacher; also includes a special Pre-K section.

www.projectaces.com

Project ACES (All Children Exercising Simultaneously). To recognize National Physical Fitness Day in May, all children exercise at a specific time on the first Wednesday in May.

www.spriproducts.com

SPRI is a fitness products catalog company specializing in rubberized tubing for resistance exercise; features toners, bands, and Xertubes for young children.

www.sportime.com

Sportime is a leading physical activity equipment company that offers a catalog with a section for young children.

www.thewiggles.com

"The Wiggles" is a popular TV show promoting music, dance, and physical activity.

www.tvturnoff.org

Includes a complete guide to organizing a TV-Turnoff Week. Send for the complete kit, which provides forms, letters to be sent home, and suggested activities.

www.yogasite.com

The Yoga Site includes a section for young children that shows graphics of postures specific to this age group.

Appendix C
Contraindicated Exercises

Contraindicated exercises are movements or exercises that may cause harm to the body. Often specific exercises will place excessive stress on the developing musculoskeletal system.

Try to avoid the following exercises. Instead use the exercises described in chapter 5 to enhance flexibility.

◄ **ARM CIRCLES.**
Problem: Forward giant arm circles with palms facing down stress the shoulder ligaments and joint. Perform with palms up and rotate arms backward.

BACK BEND. ▷
Problem: Places undue stress on the middle and lower back.

◁ **FULL SQUATS.** Problem: Place undue stress on knee ligaments.

HURDLER'S STRETCH. ▷
Problem: Places undue stress on the ligaments of the bent knee.

LEG LIFTS. ▶
Problem: Double leg lifts cause stress on the lower back.

◀ **NECK CIRCLES.** Problem: Places undue stress on the nerves and disks of the neck.

▲ **THE SWAN.** Problem: Places undue stress on middle and lower back, causing nerve pressure and disk compression.

WINDMILL. ▶
Problem: Places undue stress on
the lower back.

◀ **W-SEAT.** Problem:
Places undue stress on
the knees.

△ **YOGA PLOW.** Problem: Places undue stress on the neck.

Glossary

ballistic stretching—Bouncing or making quick jerking movements while performing a flexibility exercise.

body composition—The ratio of body fat to lean body tissue such as muscle, bone, and internal organs.

cardiorespiratory endurance (CRE)—The capacity of the heart, blood vessels, and lungs to deliver nutrients and oxygen to the tissues and remove waste products, providing energy for endurance activities (e.g., jogging, biking).

contraindicated exercises—Exercises or physical movements that are not recommended because of their potential for harm.

cool-down—The gradual lowering of physical activity levels to help the large muscles of the body return blood to the heart at a moderate rate.

flexibility—The ability to move the joints in an unrestricted fashion through a full range of motion.

fundamental movement skills—Basic movement patterns involving locomotor, nonlocomotor, and manipulative skills.

games of low organization—Activities that have simple rules and minimal playing strategies, include a few basic skills, and are easily organized.

health-related physical fitness—Components of physical fitness that have a direct impact on promoting health and well-being: cardiorespiratory fitness, muscular fitness, flexibility, and body composition.

hoppity hops—Large plastic balls with handles on which children can sit and bounce.

locomotor skills—Large-muscle skills involving a change of direction of the total body (e.g., walking, skipping).

lummi sticks—Sticks about 10 to 12 inches (25 to 30 centimeters) in length used to create a beat or rhythmic sound; often called rhythm sticks, they can be made of plastic, wood, or newspaper.

main event—An activity that includes a high level of physical exertion. It is the main focus of a physical activity session such as a game, skill activity, dance, or exercise routine to music.

manipulative skills—Motor skills in which the objective is to control one or more objects with the hands or feet (e.g., dribbling a ball, kicking a ball).

medicine balls—Weighted balls of various sizes, weights, and colors used to help develop muscular fitness. Use of medicine balls requires close adult supervision.

movement concepts—Center on how a movement is performed through the elements of space awareness, effort, and relationships.

movement themes—Center on movements that are performed or executed; classified into three areas: locomotor, nonlocomotor, and manipulative skills.

muscular endurance—The capacity of a muscle or muscle group to exert force over a period of time against a resistance that is less than the maximum you can move.

muscular fitness—Resistance exercises consisting of two major components: muscular strength and muscular endurance.

muscular strength—The capacity of a muscle or muscle group to exert maximum force against a resistance. Strength exercises using maximum resistance may be unsafe and are not recommended for children ages two to six.

nonlocomotor skills—Various movements of the body performed from a stationary base (e.g., bending, twisting, turning, balancing, stretching, and pushing).

parachute—Popular piece of equipment for children made in various textures, sizes, and colors. Parachute activities are excellent for building muscular fitness, rhythmic skills, and cooperation.

physical activity—Any body movement produced by skeletal muscles that results in energy expenditure.

play—How young children physically explore their environment to facilitate language, creativity, and social skills. Play may or may not include vigorous physical activity.

poly spots—Rubberized, disk-shaped materials that adhere to the floor to mark a spot.

repetitions—The number of consecutive times an exercise or muscle contraction is repeated.

rubberized resistance equipment—Lightweight, durable rubber tubes with handles that help promote muscular fitness. The tubes are color-coded to denote various resistance levels. Chapter 5 describes three types of tubing: the Xertube, QuickFit Toners, and the band (without handles). Use of this equipment requires close adult supervision.

sets—Specific numbers of repetitions for an exercise.

spider balls—Rubber balls with several rubber spindles protruding from the base in a random arrangement.

stability balls—Colorful, pliable balls about 14 to 18 inches (35 to 45 centimeters) in diameter that are used by young children to enhance flexibility, muscular fitness, balance, and posture.

static stretching—Maintaining a slow but steady stretch of a muscle group to a hold or stable position.

streamers—Implements used for various manipulative skills; they typically have plastic or paper handles with 3 to 4 feet (1 to 1.2 meters) of plastic or crepe paper ribbons attached to the top.

structured physical activity—Developmental activity that is planned and supervised by a parent, caregiver, or teacher.

unstructured physical activity—Child-initiated physical activity in which choice, freedom, and exploration are developed as the child moves throughout his or her environment.

warm-up—The initial portion of a physical activity session used to prepare the heart, muscles, and joints for the main event or more vigorous activity.

Bibliography

American College of Sports Medicine. 2005. *ACSM's Guidelines for Exercise, Testing, and Prescription.* 7th Ed. Philadelphia: Lippincott Williams & Wilkins.

American Heart Association. 2004. *The New American Heart Association Cookbook.* 7th Ed. New York: Author.

Berenson, G.S., et al. 1998a. Artherosclerosis: A nutritional disease of childhood. *American Journal of Cardiology* 82(10B): 22-29.

Berenson, G.S., et al. 1998b. Association between multiple cardiovascular risk factors and artherosclerosis in children and young adults: The Bogalusa Heart Study. *New England Journal of Medicine* 338(23): 1650-1656.

Berenson, G.S., et al. 1998c. *Health Ahead/Heart Smart. Curriculum Guides K-6.* New Orleans: Tulane Center for Cardiovascular Health.

Berenson, G.S., et al. 1998d. *Introduction of Comprehensive Health Promotion for Elementary Schools. The Health Ahead/Heart Smart Program.* New York: Vantage Press.

Bersma, D., and Visscher, M. 2003. *Yoga Games for Children.* Alameda, CA: Hunter House.

Bredekamp, S., and Copple, C. (Eds.). 1997. *Developmentally Appropriate Practice in Early Childhood Programs.* Washington, D.C.: National Association for the Education of Young Children.

Centers for Disease Control and Prevention. 2002. *Prevalence of Overweight Among Children and Adolescents: United States, 1999.* Atlanta: National Center for Health Statistics.

Centers for Disease Control and Prevention. 1996. *Physical Activity and Health: A Report of the Surgeon General.* Atlanta: Department of Health and Human Services.

Cone, T.P., and Cone, S.L. 2005. *Teaching Children Dance.* 2nd Ed. Champaign, IL: Human Kinetics.

Corbin, C.B., et al. 2005. *Concepts of Physical Fitness.* 12th Ed. New York: McGraw Hill.

Dishman, R.K., et al. 2004. *Physical Activity Epidemiology.* Champaign, IL: Human Kinetics.

Endres, J.B., and Rockwell, R.E. 1994. *Food, Nutrition and the Young Child.* 4th Ed. Englewood Cliffs, NJ: Prentice Hall.

Faigenbaum, A.T. 2001. Strength training and children's health. *Journal of Physical Education, Recreation and Dance* 72(3): 24-30.

Graham, G., et al. 2001. *Children Moving: A Reflective Approach to Teaching Physical Education.* 5th Ed. New York: McGraw Hill.

Hengstman, J.G. 2001. *Movement ABCs.* Champaign, IL: Human Kinetics.

Henner, M. 2001. *Healthy Kids.* New York: Harper Collins.

Insel, P., et al. 2003. *Discovering Nutrition.* American Dietetic Association. Sudbury, MA: Jones and Bartlett.

Kassing, G., and Jay, D.M. 2003. *Dance Teaching Methods and Curriculum Design.* Champaign, IL: Human Kinetics.

Kovar, S., et al. 2004. *Elementary Classroom Teachers as Movement Educators.* New York: McGraw Hill.

Lark, L. 2003. *Yoga for Kids.* Buffalo: Firefly Books.

Luby, T. 1998. *Children's Book of Yoga: Games and Exercises Mimic Plants, Animals, and Objects.* Santa Fe, NM: Clear Light.

McCall, R.M., and Craft, D.H. 2000. *Moving With a Purpose.* Champaign, IL: Human Kinetics.

Morris, L.R., and Schulz, L. 1989. *Creative Play Activities for Children with Disabilities.* Champaign, IL: Human Kinetics.

National Association for Sport and Physical Education. 2005. *Physical Best Activity Guide: Elementary Level.* 2nd Ed. Champaign, IL: Human Kinetics.

National Association for Sport and Physical Education. 2004a. *Moving Into the Future: National Standards for Physical Education.* St. Louis: Mosby.

National Association for Sport and Physical Education. 2004b. *Physical Activity for Children: A Statement of Guidelines.* 2nd Ed. Reston, VA: AAHPERD.

National Association for Sport and Physical Education. 2002. *Active Start: A Statement of Guidelines for Children Birth to Five Years.* Reston, VA: AAHPERD.

National Association for Sport and Physical Education. 2000. *Appropriate Practices in Movement Programs for Young Children, Ages 3-5.* Reston, VA: AAHPERD.

National Association for Sport and Physical Education. 1992a. *Outcomes of Quality Physical Education.* Reston, VA: AAHPERD.

National Association for Sport and Physical Education. 1992b. *What Is a Physically Educated Person? Definitions, Outcomes and Benchmarks.* Reston, VA: AAHPERD.

National Association for the Education of Young Children. 1997. Position statement on developmentally appropriate practice in early childhood programs serving children from birth to age 8. In S. Bredekamp and C. Copple (Eds.), *Developmentally Appropriate Practice in Early Childhood Programs,* Revised Ed., 3-30. Washington, D.C.: Author.

National Center for Health Statistics. 2004. *Health, United States, 2004, With Chartbook on Trends in the Health of Americans.* Hyattsville, MD: U.S. Department of Health and Human Services, CDC, NCHS.

Ogden, C.L., Flegal, K.M., Carroll, M.D., and Johnson, C.L. 2002. Prevalence and trends in overweight among US children and adolescents, 1999-2000. *Journal of the American Medical Association* 288: 1728-1732.

Pangrazi, R.P. 2004. *Dynamic Physical Education for Elementary School Children.* 14th Ed. San Francisco: Pearson Education.

Pica, R. 2004. *Experiences in Movement: Birth to Age Eight.* Clifton Park, NY: Delmar Learning.

Pica, R. 2000. *Moving and Learning Series: Toddlers.* Clifton Park, NY: Delmar Learning.

Sanders, S.W. 2002. *Active for Life.* Washington, D.C.: National Association for the Education of Young Children.

Siedentop, D. 2004. *Introduction to Physical Education, Fitness, and Sport.* 5th Ed. New York: McGraw Hill.

Spalding, A., et al. 1999. *Kids on the Ball.* Champaign, IL: Human Kinetics.

Sweet, J. 2001. *365 Activities for Fitness, Food, and Fun for the Whole Family.* New York: Contemporary Books.

Swinney, B. 1999. *Healthy Food for Healthy Kids.* New York: Meadowbrook Press.

Thomas, K.T., et al. 2003. *Physical Education Methods for Elementary Teachers.* Champaign, IL: Human Kinetics.

U.S. Department of Health and Human Services. 2000. *Healthy People 2010.* Washington, DC: Author.

Virgilio, S.J. 2000. Physical activity motivation: The missing link. *Teaching Elementary Physical Education* 11(2): 5-7, 11.

Virgilio, S.J. 1997. *Fitness Education for Children: A Team Approach.* Champaign, IL: Human Kinetics.

Virgilio, S.J. 1990. A model for parental involvement in physical education. *Journal of Physical Education, Recreation and Dance* 69(18): 66-70.

About the Author

Stephen J. Virgilio, PhD, is a professor and director of graduate studies at Adelphi University in Garden City, New York. He has researched and taught the issues surrounding children's health for more than 25 years and has served as a consultant to companies such as Fisher-Price, Sport-Fun, and Dannon Yogurt as well as to school districts across the country. Dr. Virgilio codeveloped and authored the nationally known Heart Smart Program, a comprehensive health-intervention project at the elementary school level. He also served as the coauthor of the National Association for Sport and Physical Education's (NASPE) Active Start Guidelines and wrote *Fitness Education for Children,* a book that teaches health-related fitness at the elementary school level. Dr. Virgilio has been quoted in numerous publications, including the *LA Times, Chicago Tribune,* and *USA Today* newspapers, as well as *Child* and *Parenting* magazines. He also has been a guest on several national broadcasts, including the radio program *Parent Talk* and ABC's *20/20.* Since 1977, he has been a member of NASPE and the American Alliance for Health, Physical Education, Recreation and Dance (AAHPERD). Dr. Virgilio resides with his wife, Irene, in East Williston, New York.